Social Media Marketing

Upgraded 2020

Strategies and techniques for companies

By

DOUGLAS WELCH

© Copyright 2020 by DOUGLAS WELCH'

All rights reserved.

This document is geared towards providing exact and reliable information with regards to the topic and issue covered. The publication is sold with the idea that the publisher is not required to render accounting, officially permitted, or otherwise, qualified services. If advice is necessary, legal or professional, a practiced individual in the profession should be ordered.

- From a Declaration of Principles which was accepted and approved equally by a Committee of the American Bar Association and a Committee of Publishers and Associations.

In no way is it legal to reproduce, duplicate, or transmit any part of this document in either electronic means or in printed format. Recording of this publication is strictly prohibited and any storage of this document is not allowed unless with written permission from the publisher. All rights reserved.

The information provided herein is stated to be truthful and consistent, in that any liability, in terms of inattention or otherwise, by any usage or abuse of any policies, processes, or directions contained within is the solitary and utter responsibility of the recipient reader. Under no circumstances will any legal responsibility or blame be held against the publisher for any reparation, damages, or monetary loss due to the information herein, either directly or indirectly.

Respective authors own all copyrights not held by the publisher.

The information herein is offered for informational purposes solely, and is universal as so. The presentation of the information is without contract or any type of guarantee assurance.

The trademarks that are used are without any consent, and the publication of the trademark is without permission or backing by the trademark owner. All trademarks and brands within this book are for clarifying purposes only and are the owned by the owners themselves, not affiliated with this document

TABLE OF CONTENT

Copyright..2

Introduction 5

Chapter One

Social-Media Marketing Strategies for Companies 7

Essential Elements of a Social Media Marketing Strategy 11

Marketing Strategies to Fuel Your Business Growth 16

Top 10 Tips on Collaborating With Influencers in 2020 22

Strategy Must Drive Your Social Media Marketing 25

The Benefits of Developing Adept Social Media Marketing Strategy.............31

Chapter Two

The Great Impacts of Incorporating Social Media Marketing Strategies 34

Common Social Media Marketing Challenges and Their Solutions 35

The Five Core Pillars of Social Media Marketing 37

Ways to Upgrade Your Social Media Marketing Strategy in 2020 40

How to Create a Lead Magnet That Actually Gets Leads 45

Chapter Three

Rules for Leveraging Social Media to Grow Your Business 47

How to Use Social Media to Increase Profits 50

Ways Businesses Can Use Social Media as a Tool for Progress 52

Social Media Marketing

Best Social Media Channels for Business Marketing 54

Tips for Making Social Media Work for Your Business 56

Why You Should Use Social Media for Your Business 61

Chapter Four

Essentials to Building Your Brand on Social Media 65

Advantages of Social Media Marketing for Your Business 68

Tips to Quickly Master Social Media For Businesses & Entrepreneurs 74

Creative Ways to Boost Your Social Media Strategy 79

Do's and 4 Don'ts for Businesses Using Social Media 82

Chapter Five

Steps to Productive Business Use of Social Media 85

Tips to Grow Your Business Using Social Media 87

Social Media marketing Secrets That No Marketer Will Admit To................89

Tips for Running Your Best Social Media Campaign Ever 92

Ways to Win on Promoting Your Brand Content 95

Laws of Social Media Marketing 98

Conclusion...101

INTRODUCTION

Social media marketing is a mechanism that empowers individuals to advertise their blogs, goods, or services through online social networks and to connect and reach into a much larger community that might not have been possible via traditional advertising platforms. Most importantly, social media highlights the collective rather than the individual. Throughout the Internet, communities exist in different shapes and sizes, and people talk to each other. It is the job of social media marketers to properly leverage these communities to effectively communicate relevant product and service offerings with community participants. Social media marketing also includes listening to the groups as well as establishing relationships with them as the client members. This is not always the simplest feat, as we will explore later in this novel.

Social media is essentially a communication and sharing site, fuelled by resources like those listed above. While one of social media's big applications is to keep in touch with friends and relatives around the world, it is also a medium for consumers, advertisers and staff to connect with each other, and this is where the large and ever-growing social media marketing industry comes in.

Social media marketing is the use of social media platforms to communicate with your customers and create your brand, boost sales and drive traffic to websites. This involves publishing great content on your social media profiles, listening to your followers and engaging them, analyzing your results, and running social media ads.

The main (currently) social media platforms include Facebook, Instagram, Twitter, LinkedIn, Pinterest, YouTube and Snapchat. There are also a number of social media management tools that help companies make the most of the social media platforms. Social media marketing, for example, started first with printing. In order to generate traffic to their websites and, hopefully, sales, businesses shared their content on social media. Yet social media has evolved far beyond simply being a venue to distribute content.

Nowadays, companies use a myriad of different ways of using social media. For example, a company that is concerned about what people feel about its brand should track discussions on social media and respond to specific mentions (social media listening and engagement). A business that wants to learn how it does on social media with an analytics platform (social media analytics) will evaluate its presence, interaction and revenue on social media. A company that wants to reach a specific audience on a scale would run highly targeted social media ads (social media ads). Those are also often referred to as social media management as a whole.

CHAPTER ONE

Social-Media Marketing Strategies for Companies

Social media is crucial for the success of the digital marketing strategy of any enterprise. Nevertheless, marketers of all types and sizes do not use this method to its full potential. Although the number of "follows," "likes" and "shares" is still significant, much more determines a brand's reputation than just that. Social media today requires a unique set of skills that marketers need to fully understand their audience's needs. Whether you're a young entrepreneur or a well-established brand, here are the social media tactics you need to adopt this year.

1. Continue using chatbots

You may already have learned, but there are chatbots in. This comes as no surprise since they are the only interactive device that can connect and solve problems for your consumers without any human interference being required. Besides the aforementioned, chatbots communicate with the channels through which users now feel the most relaxed interacting: social media. Platforms like Chattypeople make it easy to incorporate an AI-fueled chatbot into your social media strategy.

This tools allow you to create a chatbot that does:

- ❖ No coding expertise is needed.
- ❖ Can answer questions from consumers.
- ❖ Is able to take orders and comments directly from Facebook Messenger.
- ❖ Fits into all major payment systems.

2. Build a tailored experience for your customers

Chatbots are not just a great way to simplify those daily tasks, and if properly implemented, the chatbot will allow you to build more personalized experiences for your customers. Stop linking your advertising exclusively to your landing pages, and create ads that guide your audience with your chatbot to a Messenger portal.

Linking ads to your chatbot will:

- ❖ Split consumers ' traditional views of you trying to sell them.
- ❖ Make the experience of your Customer more unique.
- ❖ Increase sales.
- ❖ Build faithful fan base.

3. Create an efficient marketing strategy for content

Quality is key and content is no exception. Content marketing has long been a prominent form of marketing and this is not set to change in the near future. Many brands do not link quality content to the correct posting schedule, and the correct posting frequency. High-quality SEO content combined with all of the above will help you get the right customers in the right moment. Apart from its potential to draw an existing audience, a good marketing plan for advertising can be applied free of charge. Along with your structured and comprehensive content, make sure to create a related hashtag strategy.

4. Build a group for your audience

While "followers" and the many other metrics are important to social media performance, they are not the "be all and end all." You need to show the public that you're not just a robot. Integrate individuality into your posts by humour and feelings, so that your followers can respond to your brand. Social media is all about being social, and if your customers repeatedly see the same types of posts, they will lose interest.

Make interactive your communications by:

- ❖ Asking questions from your audience.
- ❖ Collecting their views on certain matters.

- Share information deserving of coverage, rather than just knowledge about your products or services.
- Like and retweet some of their stories, instead of just the other way around.
- Ask them to interact with your posts directly through "likes" and "shares"

5. Jazz up your profiles with a varied content strategy

Once and for a while, people respond to good images, fun videos and some interesting podcasts. Jazz up the content with regular usage of this type of media. If all you write and retweet is email, your social media pages can look bland so be sure to use other media types to catch your audience's attention. This is also a great way to add to your company a degree of personality.

6. Using label advocates

The people who love your brand are your greatest promotional tool. Rather than spending all of your attention on finding new clients, why not exploit the existing ones? You could use your own employees, in addition to your current customers.

To use your staff as ambassadors for the brand, you should:

- Build brand-specific social media rules.
- Tell your advocates about best practices on social media.
- Add a leader to your Social Media advocacy plan for each section.
- Track accurate data to identify areas for improvement and those that do well.

7. Create accounts on the respective channels

Now, people create profiles on every available social media site to meet as many people as possible. Unfortunately you will not hit your desired target audience with that attitude. As a consequence, when picking your social media channels, it is important that you look at your buyer's men. Of eg, if you are starting a gothic clothing brand, you won't necessarily need a LinkedIn profile; just as you won't need to be on Pinterest to advertise your surveillance services.

Social Media Marketing

8. Establish a social media budget

Social media platforms are one of the most important ways of communication, if not the most important. It is important for your performance to devote the correct budget to your social media activities. Not only this, it will be the most cost-effective way for you to meet your target audience by maximizing your budget with the right strategy. Since social media is used on a much more personal level, you will also find that it is a platform where you can communicate with your clients in a much deeper way.

9. Cross-channel promotions

Execute cross-channel campaigns across all the social media channels to further reach your clients. Keep in mind that practically every company runs these campaigns today, so you'll need to give yourself an edge to help you stand out from the crowd. Fill in your social media campaigns with an emotional component so that your viewers can respond to your cause.

An successful social media campaign across the web will be:

- ❖ Tell an entertaining story.
- ❖ Return to a particular landing page to provide more information about your campaign to your target.
- ❖ Have a catchy and exclusive name combined with related hashtags.

10. Say a story by going live

Yes, your content will tell the story of your brand as a whole, but why not share what's happening to your company in real time with your audience? Among other sites, Facebook and Instagram have developed their own live streaming apps, something that big brands are not yet using to its full potential. Start using those live features to compete with them before they really catch on.

Live stories are a great way to:

- ❖ Show your audience that you're more than just a cash machine.
- ❖ Engage your clients, and inspire them.
- ❖ Create memorable and shareable content.

Businesses around the world are slowly getting more concerned with gathering customers on their social media platforms than with their websites. You will not only set yourself up to compete with well-established brands by following these strategies outlined above, but also create a social media plan that will withstand the test of time.

Essential Elements of a Social Media Marketing Strategy

Want help getting started with your marketing strategy for social media? Would you know what to add? Targets and targets drive your social media strategy and help you communicate with your consumers effectively.

1: Identify Business Objectives

Each piece of your social media strategy meets your objectives. By understanding what you are aiming for, you really cannot push on. Look closely at the general needs of your company to determine how to use social media to help meet them. They should undoubtedly come up with several different targets, but there are a few that all businesses will integrate into their strategy— increasing brand recognition, attracting consumers and that marketing costs are important to everyone. I recommend you pick two primary goals to work on and two secondary goals. You're distracted by having too many goals and you'll end up achieving none.

2: Set Marketing Objectives

Goals aren't terribly useful if you don't have specific parameters defining when each is reached. For examples, if one of your primary objectives is to generate leads and sales, how many leads and sales do you need to generate before you find that target to be a success?

Marketing goals describe how you get from point A (an unfulfilled goal) to point B (a goal that has been achieved successfully). With the S-M-A-R-T strategy, you will decide your objectives: make your goals concrete, observable, realistic, appropriate and timely.

If your goal is to generate leads and sales, a particular marketing goal may be to increase leads by 50%. Choose which monitoring and analysis systems you need to have in order to monitor your success. It's never a good idea to set yourself up for disappointment. When you set a goal of 1.000 percent higher revenue, it's unlikely that you'll achieve it. Given the resources you have, choose goals you can achieve.

You took the time to customize your priorities so that they are applicable to your business, so apply that same attention to your targets. To get approval from your C-level executives, make sure that your priorities are important to the overall vision of the organization. It is important to set a timeline for your activities. When do you plan on completing yourgoal(s)? Next month, then? Till the end of the year?

Your target of increasing leads by 50 percent may be specific, measurable, achievable, and relevant, but if you do not set a deadline for achieving the goal, your efforts, resources, and attention may be pulled in other directions.

3: Identify Ideal Customers

If a company suffers from a poor level of commitment to its social profiles, it is typically because it lacks an authentic, ideal customer profile. Buyer people help you identify and target the right people in the right place at the right times with the right messages.

Social Media Marketing

It's easier and less expensive to reach your target audience in social media or any newspapers, if you know your age, career, wealth, desire, suffering, challenges, barriers, behaviours, likings, dislikes, motives and objections. The more detailed you are, the more clicks you get from every channel you use for your brand promotion.

4: Study Competition

When it comes to social media marketing, studying your competition not only gives you an insight into their operation, it also gives you an idea of what works so that you can incorporate such effective strategies into your own activities. Start by compiling a list of 3-5 main competitors minimum. Search which social networks they use, and analyze their strategy for content. Look at their fans or followers number, posting frequency and time of day.

Always look out for the type of content they share and its meaning (humorous, advertising, etc.) and how they react to their followers. Engagement is the most critical thing to look to. Even though page administrators are the only ones capable of measuring the rate of interaction on a single post, you can get a good idea of what they see.

Let's presume you are looking at the last 20-30 Facebook updates from a rival, for instance. Take for these posts the total number of engagement activities and divide them by the total number of fans on the page. (Engagement includes likes, comments, shares, etc.) You can use this formula on all the social profiles of your competitors (e.g. you can calculate retweets and favorites on Twitter).

Keep in mind that the measure is intended to give you a general picture of how the competition is doing so that you can compare how you are stacking up against each other.

5: Select Channels and Tactics

Most organizations build profiles on every popular social network after studying which channel can produce the most returns. By using the details from your customer personas, you can stop wasting your time in the wrong place to determine which platform is right for you.

If your prospects or clients inform you that they spend 40% of their internet time on Facebook, and 20% on Twitter, you know which primary and secondary social networks you will rely on.

This is where you need to be when your customers use a specific network — not everywhere else. Your tactics are based on your goals and objectives for each social channel, as well as on the best practices of each platform.

For example, if your goal is increasing leads and your primary social network is Facebook, some effective tactics are investing in advertising or promotional campaigns on Facebook to draw more attention to your lead magnets.

6: Build a Content Strategy

Content and social media have a symbiotic relationship: social media is worthless without great content and no one understands the content without social media. Use them together to reach your prospects, and convert them.

Each successful social media content campaign has three main components: form of content, time of posting, and duration of posting. The type of content that you should post on each social network is form and context based. Type is how this information is presented — text only, images, connections, video, etc.

Scope suits with the voice and network patterns in your business. Does your content have to be funny, serious, highly detailed and educational or anything? There's plenty of surveys that give you a specific time to post on social media. I recommend, however, that those findings be used as recommendations rather than as hard rules.

Note, the crowd is special, so you've got to check yourself to figure out the best way.

The frequency of posting is as important as the content which you share. You don't want your fans or followers to get annoyed, would you? It is important to find the perfect level because it could mean more interaction with your posts, or more unlikes and unfollows. Use Facebook Insights to see when your fans are online and how your content is engaging.

7: Allocate budget and resources

Consider the strategies you have selected to accomplish your corporate goals and objectives in order to prepare for social media marketing.

Create a comprehensive list of tools (e.g. social media tracking, email and CRM), the companies you are selling (e.g. graphic design or video production), and any commercials you are purchasing. Add next to each the estimated costs so that you have a high-quality view of what you are spending in and how your marketing budget is impacted.

Next, several businesses determine a budget, and then choose which strategies match the budget. I take a different approach. Next I draw up a strategy, and then I decide the budget that suits the strategy.

If your implementation plan costs surpass your estimation of the budget, allocate your strategies according to the timeline for ROI. Priority is given to tactics with the highest ROI (e.g. advertisement and social referral), as they produce instant profit that you can then spend in long-term tactics (fan development, quality content production or long-term commitment).

8: Assign Roles:

knowledge of who is responsible for what improves efficiency, to avoid confusion and duplication activities. Things may initially be a bit messy, but members of the time team will know their roles and what daily tasks they are responsible for.

It is time to start planning the implementation process, when everyone knows their position. You can plan either daily or weekly. I don't recommend putting together a monthly plan, because a lot of things will come up and you might end up wasting time adapting to the new changes.

Your marketing strategy on social media isn't written in stone. When you advance, you can find that some tactics don't work as well as you thought they would. Also try to adapt easily to your overall strategy and introduce the new improvements.

Marketing Strategies to Fuel Your Business Growth

It's not easy growing a business. First, you have to have a viable idea. You need to discover a profitable niche from there, define a demographic target and have something of value for selling it. Whether you're peddling products, services or information, it has become increasingly burdensome to get the word out. And without the right marketing tactics to boost your production, it's virtually impossible to turn a profit and stay afloat.

Nonetheless, the definition of the best tactics for selling your company is often contrasted with rocket science. How do you get your message to and do it effectively for the right audience? How do you improve the exposure and sales while retaining a profit with a selling offer? Today, with so much struggling from social media for our attention to search engine optimization, blogging, and pay-per-click advertising, it's easy to see why most are willing to pull their hair out.

The truth is that what has got you in business to this point will probably not get you to the next levelMost companies work "on" their companies to such an extent that they don't "on" their companies.

With a day-to-day business dealing with customer support, supply chain requirements and more, we often neglect to follow the appropriate marketing strategies, which help drive our company's growth.

What is it important to do this? Just put, you must take a step back for a moment. You must analyze and understand the basic mechanics of your message and how you can reach a wider audience without losing your shirt effectively. The key? Whatever marketing strategy you use, you will just throw away money if you don't have an effective funnel and automate your transactions.

What marketing strategies are better to use?

Many companies face a conundrum. This is aCatch-22. There is a strong need for increased visibility to boost the revenue significantly. But businesses have to spend more money to get more visibility. What are you supposed to do when that well runs dry?

There is no clear and obvious answer to that question which covers all situations. Today, though, we can do something to attract more clients even on a shoestring budget without breaking the bank. But all boils down to time. If you lose the money, you will definitely have time to improve sweat capital.

Until the foundations of a sound business are established and until you are relentless, by genuinely trying to add value, to create a meaningful relationship with the customer, there are go-to tactics to sell your business online.

1. Use social media: The social media cannot be ignored. There's all the so-called stuff going on. Several companies were built on the back of social media alone. At first it can be teasing. Clearly. But as you build momentum, you'll find it easier and easier to get posted on social media over time.

Of course, if you have money to burn, you might hire a social media manager too. But if you're not, then just be yourself. Be genuine. Make your thoughts posted. Upload the favorite goods.

Make everything you believe to be relevant and useful to help your audience learn more about you and your company or industry.

To communicate to other successful businesses use straight-for-all posts on sites such As Facebook, Snapchat or Twitter or even to possibly consumers searching their products and services. This marketing is very powerful.

2. Making video tutorials: The development of video tutorials is one of the most effective ways to get the word out on your business. Provide something useful to people. Let them step through it. Keep your hands up. The videos are all the rage. The stronger you are at this, the easier you can increase your exposure, and eventually your profits, the more interest you have.

Today, behind Google, YouTube is the world's second largest search engine. They head over there whenever someone wants to visually learn something. You have probably done it countless times on yourself. So just ask yourself what you can do in your business to help customers overcome a certain pain point? Next, what got you into business?

Most tough part? Hearing back your own voice and even seeing yourself. You don't need to physically appear on camera yet, but you'll still need to be noticed. Over time you become used to it. Yet you can't ignore YouTube's popularity and scope so get out there and start making now, right now, real and usable videos.

3. Start writing now: You should definitely start a blog. If you don't have a blog for your business then immediately start one. But not just writing on your own account. Many people find blogging boring because the exposure is low. The reality is that your blog will be like a desolate wasteland unless you are mindful of what you are doing.

But this is not just about posting your ideas on a blog of your own. You should start blogging on authority. Post content using platforms such as Medium. Reply to questions on Quora and Reddit. Or move out onto the publishing platform of

LinkedIn. These are all platforms of authority on which anyone can publish, which have huge crowds, allowing you to enter quickly and instantly.

Make sure you blog effectively when you do blog. Don't post subtle content. Just think of adding value. Worried about all the corporate secrets being revealed? Don't be so. Give the Farm away. Give people so much value that, in their eyes, you immediately become an authority. It's one of the strongest strategies you can use to market any business.

4. Understand search engine optimisation: I am incredibly passionate about this marketing area. But it's also a place that scares other people mortally. Sure, SEO can be frightening. But that can be strong too. And when you learn to leverage it, and the right way to learn SEO, the sky is the limit.

There are businesses out there that show you how to "trick" Google using shady PBNs and other link schemes. It may have short-term results but you will land in hot water in the long run. With SEO you cannot take shortcuts. Just like in industry, if you want to see the results, you have to put in the work and the time.

Any ideas to do the right way? Don't spamboost keywords. Hands down. This is one of the most serious mistakes the people make. Create your human content, while also paying tribute to search engines. But more importantly, make sure whatever you convey is insightful, engaging, unique and adds tremendous value.

5. Leverage influencers: Do you want to get the word out there and increase your visibility on social media without having to take years to build the public? Then certainly you should leverage the influencers. But founding the right influencer is the key. You don't have to go with millions of followers who have influencers. For tens of thousands, or even a hundred thousand fans, you could opt for micro-influencers.

The trick, right? Find the right niche influencer so that you target the right audience. It's not just about getting your message across. It is about getting your message across to the right consumer base. If you can do that properly, then you can probably reach a large audience for not having invested much money when you think about the potential profit it can return.

If your distribution and marketing processes are in operation, then that makes sense. If you have an offer that is clearly converting, and it's just about more visibility, then this is probably the right marketing strategy right now for you. Assessing the situation and reaching out to influencers and gaging their price. Do small tests, then scale and see what works.

6. Construct a great lead magnet: There is a great deal of marketing efficiency to produce a big lead magnet. I found that the right lead magnet to the right audience could produce explosive results. When you are able to identify and display a cure in your lead magnet, you're on the right track.

What kind of problem do consumers have in their niche? First of all, when did you make it? Ask these questions before installing your magnet on the floor. The better the question or pressure points you recognize at the outset, the better you can fix them in your lead magnet.

How do you like to make a lead magnet? That could be an ebook, a cheat sheet, a guide, a video... Naturally, it's not only the lead magnet. To get customers into your pipeline you have to have a squeeze website and a sizzling screenshot of your sales. But all of this starts with a big lead magnet. The better, the more efficient you will be at reaching your audience.

7. Use Facebook ads with re-targeting: Facebook ads are among the most powerful methods you can use these days to market just about anything. You can reach a very specific audience with Facebook and you can do it with great ease. You may target by interest, age, status of relationships, geographic location, and so much more.

But the trick here is not just about click-traffic, to get great results. You need to concentrate on transformations and pixel re-targeting. If you don't know how to mount the Facebook Pixel on your screen, you've got to learn how to do it right now. Even if you don't run Facebook ads, with one pixel, you can build your audience.

Pixels track everybody that comes to your site, and around them you can build custom audiences. For instance, if you post content on how to learn how to drive a semi-truck and track visitors with pixels, then you can market truck driving certification to people who have already shown interest in it because they have visited that particular page. And it will skyrocket your conversions.

8. Use LinkedIn the correct way: Have you got a video on your LinkedIn profile? Knew you could easily add one? Why don't you take the time to present yourself and your business. Link that to describe your profile. This is a simple way to market your business passively, and it can lead to unexpected outcomes when done correctly.

If you have a lot of connections on LinkedIn and you don't actually posting on it, start right away. You can reach a large audience, particularly when the posts go viral. This is a great place to convey the journey of enterprise. Talk and tell stories about your challenges. The more efficient your stories become, the greater your potential reaches when you go viral.

On LinkedIn you can also reach out to other companies and collaborate with like-minded entrepreneurs. For all things business it's a great go-to resource and too many people overlook that.

9. Create an affiliate program: Most people don't understand the marketing power of affiliates. Affiliates can provide growth with massive fuel. But it's not always that easy to approach the right partners. If you want the bigger affiliate to take you seriously you must have good conversion.

I find it can be tricky to navigate the partner minefield. It takes persistence, so getting it through deserves true grit. Most of us get discouraged after a few setbacks, but when it comes to affiliate you cannot allow emotions to get in the way. Build an affiliate program and begin reaching out to a potential affiliate that can help.

10. Use Email Marketing Sequences: An email marketing sequence will be a part of any good sales funnel. These are the automatic notifications that go out to users when they sign up for your site. Use your email series to forge a subscriber partnership. Be real, and be honest. So carry on your ride.

Using email replies to segment the list, and then click. For starters, if someone clicks on a specific connection, they have obviously shown an interest in something. Label the customer later selling it to them. If somebody purchases, tag them as a buyer. Identifying your buyers and your subscribers' interests is enormous for segmentation.

Split test when you are sending broadcasts. Split test everything, in fact, before you pull the trigger and really try it out, you never really know what will be the most successful. This will help you to understand better what your audience is responding to, make you a better communicator and be better able to sell to your clients.

Top 10 Tips On Collaborating With Influencers in 2020

It is no coincidence that one of the popular marketing techniques is influencing the marketing. Working with influencers can help you market your brand more effectively with a well-developed strategy! We are seeing many new approaches coming out as marketing and social media become harmonized. Competition is rising day by day on social media platforms and content editors are becoming more valuable on digital platforms.

Many web editors also use their social media accounts to build their own target groups. They transform the accounts into commercial platforms with time and direct the communities to the accounts.

So, is there a way on the brand side to use those influencers? Yes, because they've created their own social media value now and they're sure to have a remarkable authority. Influencer marketing is a super-efficient area to get results easily and has the potential to catch the intended customers instead of trying to hope that the organic customers will proceed. Instead of standard users, users lend credit to the opinions of influencers. Since end users very much value influencers as they arrive at the decision point. Let's dig into the techniques of communication and teamwork and see how to successfully use them:

1. Investigate: Influencers on social media do not by accident or by coincidence raise their followers. We have an audience so we know what they want, evaluate them and satisfy them. Through posting, they're adopting several different and interesting tactics. So don't just pay them, and tell them to share directly your product.

To make your content more effective, count on the experience and creative talents of your influencer to the full. That is what they are doing. If you have specific needs, of course, share, but don't insist because they probably know better in this field. Because they are specialized they can take the right approach.

2. Keep an open mind about new ideas: If they hate the product, influencers won't share the product directly because they know if they share it, they lack plausibility and legitimacy with their fans. Your influencer collection is important at this point, make sure you partner with the right influencers. You are thereby with the right person to passionately present your brand / product / service.

3. Build a viable forum for win - win: While influencers with too many fans are strong on social media, they may be a bit inexperienced when it comes to brand words. They will learn in time but in the meantime you will gain profit in the long run if you support them with all the supplies, networks and competence.

4. Generate a targeted consumer base: When it comes to choosing influencers, brands have too many options, but at this point selection is important. You two will have a "causal connection" if you find an influencer that has less followers but more expertise in your field. So that means you can attract potential customers and share the deserved area of your work.

It's all about target audience.

5. Consider the brand ambassadors influencers: A classic approach is to send influencers to the sponsored events. What about managing your influencer in those events to act as a "reporter?" If your influencer has a talent like this, they trust the product / brand even more each time people see your influencer in an event.

6. Motivate influencers to make contests and create new campaigns: Brands sponsor attractive prize-winning competitions to "keep" them in the game. If influencers do the same through their brands, then the impact doubles so that they can benefit everyone in the chain.

7. Count on advantageous networking: Now there are too many brands and their equivalents and a lot of them want to communicate with the influencers. Yet because content marketing really comes and has to proceed fluently, it's important to have the right connection between each.

Make profitable connections with brands, particularly when you think it's time to execute the right promotion.

8. Trust in the decisions of influencer: influencers have become influencers because they have a clear and efficient way of approaching their fans. People are listening to them and they respect them. Because of this, they decide to set up their own business at one point of their success, and direct the others in creative markets. He pushes influencers to do the best they can to treat them the way they deserve. Otherwise, both sides could face unexpected situations.

9. Use influencers over celebrities: It seems like a good idea for the brand to make a celebrity the spokesperson for the new product launch, yet it doesn't always work. The star always steals the limelight, and the commodity is overlooked, thereby losing the money expended. Instead of using a huge celebrity, the campaign uses an expert,

Social Media Marketing

prosperous, and trusted influencer. Don't always ignore who the target group is. Keep in mind that every field authority is a social media influencer.

10. Obtain realistic targets for campaigns: The people who convince others that the perfect new idea is really good are influencers. They do this in a faster and more efficient way, and they ensure conversation through your product. Even so, this too can be overcome by a professionally made advert. How about combining the two and having more reach?

Generate content based on the user and make users a part of the campaign.

The best way to do this is to collaborate with and also find people that are oriented, so you can show to your client that you are doing this professionally and, automatically pass your message to the public. Because the influencers are much quicker and more efficient.

Strategy Must Drive Your Social Media Marketing

When it comes to your company, your social media marketing strategies must be based on a plan. If you don't have a strategy in place you're not going to make really good progress. At least not the strides you'll be making if you have the strategy that works for you.

- ❖ ***The purpose of your social media marketing campaign:*** your social media strategy acts as a roadmap to get from point A to point B. This encourages you to stay on the right direction for your company and lets you increase traffic with top-quality target audience members. If your company doesn't have a marketing strategy for social media means you won't be in charge of the path you are going to follow and exactly where you are going to end up.

It may mean you'll be all over the place and you'll be able to never (at least not all of them) achieve your goals. It is definitely important enough to exploit as intimidating as social media can be to you, because it will make the company more successful.

- ***Will social media relate the way you expect to your strategy?*** As you're designing and working on your social media marketing campaign, it's crucial that you feel confident that it really does make a positive difference for your company. In such a situation your strategy is very important and it is essential that you know exactly what you're doing and how you're going to accomplish what you're setting out to do. If you choose to delegate the social media activities of your business to someone else, if it is very important that you choose that person with great care and prudence.
- ***Planning a social media marketing plan:*** the social media marketing strategy of your company is very critical and not only do you need one, but you also need to make sure your approach is well thought out and successful. A unique methodology is one aspect of what you need to include in your social media marketing plan.

First of all, setting your goal(s) before you do anything else is critical. Without goals, you'll have a very hard time getting where you need to be. If you're trying to think about designing your plan as something fun and interesting, it's not going to become a "work" but a pleasurable experience. You'll see if you use that approach it will go smoothly and easily.

An extremely important second step is to align your social media marketing strategy with our targets. You have to make sure the two of you have an established connection. All this ties with going from point A to point B. You won't make much change without the coordination.

There are a lot of different goals for social media marketing that you can concentrate on. Some of the more productive ones are: • New lead generation.

- ❖ The number of people who opt in to your newsletter or other offerings is dramatically increasing.
- ❖ Promote a given event.
- ❖ The landing page draws more users.
- ❖ Fostering new offers.
- ❖ Pay close attention to analytics, so you can clearly understand how your business is progressing.

Providing loans where credit is due. It is very important to acknowledge your fans and followers who have been kind enough to support your efforts and pass the word on to others they know and trust. In a way, express how much you appreciate what they do for you and your business. Some of the analytics you should pay attention to are the number of conversions you made, the amount of revenue you generated through those conversions, and the total amount of money you earned through your efforts in social media marketing.

Figuring out how performance is described. It's extremely important to be able to define and measure success when it comes to your social media marketing strategy. ***There are several ways to measure that, including:***

- ❖ Stepping up the number of conversions you could make.
- ❖ Multiply the number of retweets that have happened on Facebook.
- ❖ Increasing the number of new visitors, the time spent on the website of your company and the number of times the page has been visited by visitors.

The wins your company achieves should be closely linked to your marketing activities in social media and tracked through the analytics tools. It's critical that you understand that your efforts in social media are closely tied to the success of your business.

Social Media Marketing

If you want to be professional successful you have no choice but to be as active on social media as you can. Remember that your social media marketing efforts are consistent, persistent and discrete. In the long run, that will be worth the effort. Whatever you do in company, make sure your efforts produce results that work for you.

Get More Reach With Social Media Marketing Strategies That Work for You

You probably already have your business on Facebook, Twitter, Instagram, LinkedIn and all the other platforms you need to be to reach your customers. But even so, to inspire the commitment you know you need to get, it doesn't feel like you're getting the right traction or posting the right media. In short, your marketing strategies for social media aren't well tuned and some might even say, non-existent.

1. Finding the Techniques for Your Niche

One of the major problems with the marketing strategies of many businesses is that they apply the same approaches to their social media team as a standardized response system. This means that in essence, instead of tailoring them to their specific niche or industry, they take social media marketing strategies they've heard about and use them "as is."

For example, restaurants ' social media marketing strategies will be very different from those for Fortune 500 companies ' social media marketing strategies. Naturally, when we put it that way, it seems very obvious-unfortunately, social media's constant failures let us know it's not. The problem arises because not only are each industry's outcomes and goals very different, the means to the end also have to be different.

2. Why Using This Strategy for Your Business is Vital

For example, the marketing strategies of a restaurant should be to encourage audiences to come in and eat in our case above. Which means taking photos of various dishes and sharing them on Facebook, Twitter and Instagram is a smart tactic.

This produces salivation for the food, and it is likely that people will Like, Post, Re-Tweet, etc. This leaves the restaurant fresh in the eyes of the customer and they will recall how good the food looks and make reservations every time they are looking for a place to eat.

On the other hand, from photo media, a Fortune 500 company won't get much contact. Yes, it may be interesting to talk to Bob in accounting, but an image of him studying diagrams in the breakroom on his tablet is unlikely to encourage the best kind of conversation.

That's because the priorities of a Fortune 500 social media company are likely to bring in more clients, keep current consumers interested and attract top talent for the company. The best way to do this would be to use social media marketing strategies that will establish the company as a leader in the industry. Sharing blog posts that contain relevant and useful information, for example, is a great way to market yourself as at the industry's forefront.

3. How to tailor your social media marketing strategies

With so many industries and niches out there, it would be almost impossible to go through each one, showing you how to tailor your marketing strategies to the exact niche you are looking for. Instead, going through how different targets affect your marketing strategies would be more time-efficient. Just think about what you're trying to do, and then match it with some of the suggestions that follow. Keep in mind that interaction is the ultimate short-term goal for social media, so anything that gets you to that point-no matter how strange or unconventional it might be-will be best for your business.

✓ ***Expand your Base Customer.*** If you are working through this marketing strategy to broaden your customer base, you're going to want to post content that's easily sharable and branded. It means that the more traction the posts get, and the harder it is to trace those posts back to you, the better it is for business.

A great way to do this is to post links to your blog on your website, provided that the blogs are of course high-value in terms of content and information. It encourages people to share the link to your website, which means the more viral it becomes, the more links it will bring into your website. See for sure that at the end of the blog there is a clear CTA (call to action) pointing to your contact or sales sites. If your social media marketing tactics have proved effective in the past by posting media images and video, make sure the videos are watermarked with your name.

✓ ***Strengthen your current List of Clients.*** Another great benefit of this medium is being able to reinforce the loyalty of your current clients. We all know that bringing in a new customer costs more than retaining a current one, so that's a big chunk of social media marketing strategies right here.

The key is that you want to give your customers continuous value. This means that if you're in an industry that constantly releases new information; you should be the first to provide that information to your fans. Ask yourself this: What value do I give my followers? If you cannot mention at least five items, you will start doing a better job immediately. Warn the fans about activities relating to their preferences, posting, updates, recipes, etc. Give suggestions and loose advice but stay away from risk-the bottom line here is that you want your clients to know why they need you every single day in their lives.

4. Using Your Social Media Marketing Strategies Wisely: When all of this is said and done, when it comes to social media marketing strategies, the only guidelines to follow are whatever works for you. Social media is still a fairly young advertisement tool (in contrast with Television, radio, newspaper, etc.)

So nothing is written in stone. Even the so-called "experts" in the industry are still fine-tuning their marketing strategies so you can expect things to change in the next decade or so on an almost consistent basis.

The best you can do is keep your ear to the ground and stay afloat with all the latest information, techniques and trends, until that time comes and it becomes a science.

The Benefits of Developing Adept Social Media Marketing Strategy

Social media is on a rampant upsurge. From fast correspondence to market marketing, the small businesses are now using social media to promote their brands, services and products in the most effective way. These businesses can reach out to the targeted customer base by following a strategic approach and enhance their brand visibility in the online periphery. However, social media is no longer a platform for anonymous virtual interaction, but rather a clear identity is developed for itself. Therefore, it is imperative to follow appropriate marketing strategy for SMO and create a prospective channel through which products and services can be promoted in the best possible way.

Right strategy for social media marketing is a good way to connect with targeted clients while generating better web traffic at the same time. There are different social platforms that help businesses channel the information they need, and the most popular are Twitter, Facebook, YouTube, LinkedIn, MySpace etc.

In social media marketing strategies, the companies emerging with useful information about their businesses are viable. Through providing the right content, online viewers will be able to connect and track these small businesses. The SMM approach will harp on open social networking conversations and interactions.

There should be no form of spamming or unnecessary sales pitch as this will not help to satisfy the ultimate business needs in any way.

The best way to attract potential customers and boost profits is to invest time to frame distinct social media marketing campaign. There are many strategies involving careful formulation of a policy. Social bookmarking sites, for example, play a crucial part in guiding your SMM plan. Such sites help track the target audience, download and vote for your page, thus helping you enter a wider market.

Facebook, the micro-blogging website is another powerful channel of communication to improve exposure for small businesses. Twitter provides your followers with quality information, and helps establish brand visibility for your business in the process. Twitter is one of the most important tools for social media marketing on the B2B.

In B2B social media marketing, the approach is characterized by an action plan on how you achieve the target of the company. You need to harp on certain parameters to form a good strategy as you decide to move ahead. The most important thing to consider when beginning a SMM initiative is to understand why you need media platforms to be used. Is it to build awareness of the brand; is it to increase sales to serve both of these purposes?

The next critical thing is to understand where the potential audience stands? If it is' nowhere' then your primary motive must be to notify your customers of your business. Instead slowly concentrate on engaging with the intended group of consumers and creating potential leads.

The next goal in B2B social media marketing is to find out your target audience's media interest, and how they tend to use social media. While some are browsing RSS feeds or bookmarking their favorite sites, others are just using social networking sites and video podcasting apps to track fascinating stuffs.

You need to remember that these aspects depend on specific age groups, interests, and other patterns of social behaviour, so you need to plan and strategize to work out those interests and turn them into your reward programs.

To build a strong SMM approach, you should be mindful of the specific selling proposition of your product. Not the goods you're making or distributing, but figure out that one thing makes your business special among the rivals. Defines your USP and initiates a campaign that speaks volumes about the uniqueness and draws the potential visitors attention. This is the first and most important step in awareness raising for your brand.

Fostering your media participation in real-time is very important in social media marketing strategy. Social media marketing is about gaining relationships in the online realm with prospective customers, and this can be done through interaction initiation. You need to give your targeted clients a human face to interact with. Commenting on the blogs, posting forums are some of the best ways to communicate effectively with the online public.

There's no denying that the small businesses need social media marketing to create a successful online presence. Nonetheless, formulating a plan in social media marketing is not a child's play, but needs considerable skills and hiring a professional social marketing agency is recommended for the best outcome.

CHAPTER TWO

The Great Impacts of Incorporating Social Media Marketing Strategies

Search engine optimization features are quickly adopted by modern businesses today on their websites to boost their web presence and increase web traffic for a higher bottom line. These SEO features play an important role in hiking the web site ranking by major search engines.

However, there are extra work and features to be incorporated with any successful business website on an ongoing basis for continual success. This is where active social marketing comes into play with the host of Internet marketing techniques available in the market.

1. Wide variety:

Today's progressive technology brings on a host of online advertising on the Internet platform with a variety of local display and social media advertising. These and blog writing can enhance the search engine optimization efforts of any business site dramatically through professional SEO services offered in the market.

A high ranking website is crucial to the online presence of the web business as this draws more web traffic to the targeted site. There must be the essential investment of Internet marketing services that include local search engine advertising, local display advertising and re-targeting as well as social media optimization.

2. Functionality:

There is a plethora of online sites on the Internet that can boost the presence and value of any business site. This includes the popular Twitter and Facebook which allow an unleashing of the social media websites potential through SEO experts. Regular postings and interactions with web consumers through such SEO features would bring on more online marketing successes.

Social media marketing has to do with the creation and maintenance of an active website presence on preferred social media sites to draw more web traffic. This would include the display of appropriate advertisements on these popular social sites to target at appropriate prospective customers seeking the desired products and services.

Social marketing efforts that are consistent and innovative can draw more fans and followers with the limited marketing budget.

3. Management efforts:

It may be a daunting task for some webmasters to manage their social media marketing efforts if the business is expanding or on a multinational basis. It could be that business owners or webmasters have too much on their hands to manage the business site SMO accounts; professional social media marketers can be hired to do this with more SEO services incorporated in a tailored package that would benefit the company.

Professional SEO service providers who manage the company's social media accounts can also assist in building up an appropriate online community for the business' benefit while building the page rank of the business site.

Common Social Media Marketing Challenges and Their Solutions

If your online business faces the pressure that abounds on the internet, a robust online marketing strategy will have to be put in place. Not all marketing strategies work, however, and you are bound to fall victim to some of these.

Here are some of the most common problems experienced in formulating an online marketing strategy, and how to address these challenges.

- ✓ ***Comprehension of marketing techniques***: many online businesses are attempting to use social media methods without getting the vagueest understanding of what, when, where and why. It is very important for online businesses to be able to answer the "W" questions when coming up with a concrete online marketing strategy. Through tracking social media, online businesses need to be able to understand key factors which decide how competitive the company is.

  Some of these considerations include knowledgeable comprehension, keywords important to your target audience, and branding. By not doing this, businesses that otherwise might have been very productive lose out on opportunities for sales, customer service, publicity, public relations and collaborations.

- ✓ ***Maintaining resilience:*** You need to be vigilant if you agree that your online marketing campaign would require a major contribution to social media. Online companies with the most successful blogs are the ones which always update them with new content. Heading the top is the best way to inspire consistency. You should set goals for the contributions and offer feedback. Your business will need to put aside resources for engaging, monitoring, or creating content.

- ✓ ***Data Paralysis:*** Data should always be part of the decision-making process, but creative ideas should never be stomped. Instead of waiting for data to prove a concept, it is sometimes more feasible to make use of your social media experience to come up with your online marketing strategy; as the former might be a bit restrictive.

- ✓ ***Personalization deficit:*** You should use real team members in the marketing of your business as opposed to the use of faceless people in the marketing of marks "X."

Social Media Marketing

You should focus on being useful and getting to your target audience. You should not mind putting others at the forefront in doing so. You shouldn't care about team members being really famous because eventually their loyalty will be to the brand that's good for the business.

✓ ***Digitally Savvy teams:*** In order to develop a strong online marketing strategy, you need a team of online marketers who are good at what they are doing. It's not all gloomy, however, as you can easily learn by listening, participating, training, and engaging.

The Five Core Pillars of Social Media Marketing

1. Strategy

Before you dive right in and publish something on social media, let's take a step back and look at the bigger picture. The first step is to think about your social media strategy.

What are your goals? How can social media help you achieve your business goals? Some businesses use social media for increasing their brand awareness, others use it for driving website traffic and sales. Social media can also help you generate engagement around your brand, create a community, and serve as a customer support channel for your customers.

Which social media platforms do you want to focus on? The major social media platforms, mentioned above, are Facebook, Instagram, Twitter, LinkedIn, Pinterest, YouTube, and Snapchat. There are also smaller and up-and-coming platforms, such as Tumblr, Tik Tok, and Anchor, and social messaging platforms, such as Messenger, WhatsApp, and WeChat.

When starting out, it's better to pick a few platforms that you think your target audience is on than to be on all platforms.

What type of content do you want to share? What type of content will attract your target audience best? Is it images, videos, or links? Is it educational or entertaining content? A good place to start is to create a marketing persona, which will help you answer these questions. And this doesn't have to be fixed forever; you can always change your strategy according to how your social media posts perform.

2. Planning and Publishing

Social media marketing for small businesses usually starts with having a consistent presence on social media. Close to three billion people (3,000,000,000!) use social media.

By being present on social media platforms, you give your brand an opportunity to be discovered by your future customers.

Publishing to social media is as simple as sharing a blog post, an image, or a video on a social media platform. It's just like how you would share on your personal Facebook profile. But you will want to plan your content ahead of time instead of creating and publishing content spontaneously. Also, to ensure that you are maximizing your reach on social media, you need to publish great content that your audience likes, at the right timing and frequency.

There are now a variety of social media scheduling tools that can help you publish your content automatically at your preferred time. This saves you time and allows you to reach your audience when they are most likely to engage with your content.

3. Listening and Engagement

As your business and social media following grow, conversations about your brand will also increase. People will comment on your social media posts, tag you in their social media posts, or message you directly.

People might even talk about your brand on social media without letting you know. So you will want to monitor social media conversations about your brand. If it's a positive comment, you get a chance to surprise and delight them. Otherwise, you can offer support and correct a situation before it gets worse.

You can manually check all your notifications across all the social media platforms but this isn't efficient and you won't see posts that didn't tag your business's social media profile. You can instead use a social media listening and engagement tool that aggregates all your social media mentions and messages, including posts that didn't tag your business's social media profile.

4. Analytics

Along the way, whether you are publishing content or engaging on social media, you will want to know how your social media marketing is performing. Are you reaching more people on social media than last month? How many positive mentions do you get a month? How many people used your brand's hashtag on their social media posts?

The social media platforms themselves provide a basic level of such information. To get more in-depth analytics information or to easily compare across social media platforms, you can use the wide range of social media analytics tools available.

5. Advertising

When you have more funds to grow your social media marketing, an area that you can consider is social media advertising. Social media ads allow you to reach a wider audience than those who are following you.

Social media advertising platforms are so powerful nowadays that you can specify exactly who to display your ads to. You can create target audiences based on their demographics, interests, behaviors, and more. When you are running many social media advertising campaigns at once, you can consider using a social media advertising tool to make bulk changes, automate processes, and optimize your ads.

Ways to Upgrade Your Social Media Marketing Strategy in 2020

With more than three billion people now using social media every day, keeping ahead of the curve is important when it comes to the social media practices of your company or customer.

But when social media keeps changing this can be difficult. Throughout 2018 and into 2019, there have been a host of changes on social media platforms. There are also a ton of new trends affecting how users are engaging on these platforms. Each of these changes was a catalyst for corporations to adjust their marketing strategies and tactics for social media.

You also need to change the approach to remain competitive. Here are the tactics needed by your 2020 social media strategy.

1. Target true engagement: It has been a popular social tactic for some time to cheat the system to encourage engagement, with brand sharing posts suggesting users simply "tag a friend in the comments below" to rack up figures of interaction without actually creating a conversation. Yet machines are becoming smarter, and this year's interaction bait will not make it as networks crack down on spammy schemes to win likes and shares.

With organic reach declining and more companies upping their social ad spending, content needs to be truly interesting and engaging so followers and broader audiences can't help but get involved. Whether it's irreverent conversation in MERL and Gregg's style, or creating Facebook's artistic vertical video, finding the voice and stories that work for you is more important than ever.

How to jump to the trend: Stop relying on social lazy CTAs. Think about your brand voice guidelines and how best to apply them to social media, using social as part of broader content marketing strategies rather than a stand-alone approach.

2. Working with micro-influencers: It is no wonder that micro-influencers continue to gain ground on the theme of true engagement with their more famous counterparts. In addition to the budget benefits, research continues to show that its public are more engagement and can be more niche special than singing and all-dancing social media stars, as do micro influencers who often work on a gift basis or simply have lower fees than large names.

Some analysis has shown that, once more than a few thousand users have assembled a profile, the engagement rate on sites like Instagram is rapidly diminishing. Collaboration with digital groups with 1000 to 10,000 supporters is a fraction of the normal influential rate, but is likely to result in a much greater real participation.

Some brands have turned their nose to the idea of collaboration with micro-influences, but anyone who wants to produce credible cooperation in 2018 needs to take up the ups and downs. This has been partly due to the credibility that bigger "influencers have to lose.

How to hop on trend: Take your time in your field to study up-and-comers. Check related hashtags to find social stars that are not sponsored by advertisers, where there are wider crowds and higher participation levels. Planning influencer ads focused on interest, not size of audience.

3. Get rid of fake followers: It would be unfair not to address the issue of fake social followers that really gained momentum during 2019 on the subject of true interaction and influencer marketing. Fake and spam accounts have been around since the dawn of social media, but now it's becoming increasingly common to find so-called "influencer" profiles with millions of followers, where reality isn't exactly what it seems.

Even politicians and famous people have actually been caught cheating.

The assumption that the size of the viewer does not automatically match the views or events is part of the reason why the search for participation level before communicating with the influer.

Fake followers and paid shares may make it look like someone is known, but it may waste time and money to carry out closer inspections.

2020 has already defined the year in which bogus followers are the number one public enemy and the efforts to root out fake behavior have been revealed by platforms like Instagram and Facebook.

4. Consider your social profile shoppable: The buyable Pinterest Pins to Instagram checkout have already created waves for shopping network. In the past year, though, some big changes have taken place, and the path from social framework to checkout is now easier and quicker than ever.

Pinterest has upgraded ad pins to "Product Pins"— a tool that takes shoppers straight to the checkout page for a selected item on the retailer's website, while Instagram now offers users a route from discovery to checkout without ever having to leave the app.

Even a shopping tab now features the "Explore" page— something that paid search marketers should be aware of.

Pinterest says their product pins have increased retailer website click-through rates by 40%. With shoppers likely to drop a purchase if too many steps are taken between viewing an item and paying for it, retailers should take the opportunity to make instant sales that social media encourages.

With many shoppers browsing socially or on Google for the first time, paid search and paid social teams need to work hand-in-hand throughout 2019 with a clear understanding of their respective tactics and results.

5. Include dark social in your strategy: Dark social is a social networking of information sharing via WhatsApp, Facebook Messenger, iMessage and other applications that marketers cannot track. We are increasingly aware that the content we use online is part of our very own online presence and that posts we like or comment on are published with this information in the newsfeeds of our friends. Together with an inconvenience of smart advertising and an increasing lack of faith in social media as a whole, the situation has created a great deal of unforeseeable social communication. Direct postal and product messaging may seem to be a major brand awareness hit, but that is not the case–although these types of exchanges may not be trackable, they promote valuable commitment.

Facebook's Messenger app has 1.3 billion people sending 8 billion messages per month, and a peak of about 5 billion active monthly users once you include WhatsApp, WeChat and Skype. That's more than the entire traditional social networks, suggesting "shadow media" can not necessarily be ignored as an environment that advertisers cannot reach. Overall, 75 per cent of consumer sharing is estimated to occur on the dark social.

6. Capitalize on FOMO with live video

Tired of hearing about millennial? Well, because you should turn your attention this year to Generation Z. Generation Z members are now starting their careers, usually named "born" between 1995 and 2015 and look at where they spend their own disposable income. The fear of lack inspires experiential marketing experiences and content campaigns generated by the user in this age group. FOMO

Socially speaking, digital marketing has to have the same attitude that you miss with pop-up stores and one-off events. Live video and super-short time-sensitive tournaments are just a few ways to get FOMO into a crowd that is waiting through IGTV, Facebook Live and other Instagram platforms.

A particular benefit of live videos lies in the fact that followers on a wide variety of sites are alerted anytime they watch someone go live— a good way to escape processes that minimize organic content.How to hop on trend: Fine-tune a live video plan and execute it. Research the customers deeply to consider what they want, and use elements such as images behind the scenes, interviews with insiders and giveaways to keep people involved.

7. Augmented reality advertisements are being tested: Increased reality is already creating waves of customer experience, which are used in apps that help users wear lipsticks and sunglasses, or imagine how a paint color could feel at their living room. Facebook has already developed AR-ready ads, which allow users to select the product ad and experience the article without leaving any news feed.

Yet Snapchat has long led the way, giving advertisers with customized selfie filters and stickers the opportunity to reach customers.

Some have proclaimed Augmented Reality as the future of digital marketing, though the impact it will have (at least for some time) will depend on your business. Beauty and fashion brands are the early adopters of course, with NYX, Sephora and Michael Kors already testing out the new Facebook feature.

Social media isn't just a tool to increase brand awareness, it can drive revenue and customer retention increases and help build an engaging customer experience.

"Cutting through the noise" may seem like an impossible task when every channel is so loud today, but it can be achieved with targeted marketing and a trustworthy, relatable strategy. Instead of tossing the net as wide as possible, advertisers can take the time to dig at thorough observations and get a feel for the subtle details in their audience's different sections. Where are the Micro-Marketing opportunities? Where can we get intimate without it sounding over - the-top or insincere?

The idea that publics are not just numbers on a computer is at the heart of a good social media campaign. They are people with a multitude of desires and ambitions, and if you are able to capture their attention with something really positive rather than negative, campaigns become the basis for long-term success rather than another flash in the pan.

How to Create a Lead Magnet That Actually Gets Leads

A good lead magnet produces thousands of leads a month for your company. Lead magnets are a great chance to obtain targeted leads, the ubiquitous free offerings attached to a signup form. The lead magnets can be easily created. It's difficult to create targeted lead magnets. Such tips help you overcome the difficulties of creating complex lead magnets that yield excellent results.

To provide customers with their information, you have to provide a justification. Many people today are so overloaded by emails, updates and ads that the lead magnet has to be really impressive to make people add a new account. The outcome they had once did not generate any more by asking people to sign up for your list. You need some value— namely a client's email address — in order to get something of value.

Nearly any website or email listed company uses lead magnets to attract customers to its list. However the question is not whether lead magnets attract— they do. That is the problem, how well they draw and who they attract.

Know Your Client.

All good marketing starts with getting to know your customer. Who is your Client? What is it that he or she wants, needs and wants? How can you fulfill those needs with your products or services?

The work starts when you create your lead magnet: the perfect person you would like to subscribe to your email list to define your target client will help you to refine your offer of content so that your lead magnet attracts not only a lot, but also good guidelines.

The most successful lead magnets give the customer great value while satisfying the needs or problem of a customer.

These magnets are tailored for the target audience, as they provide a much-needed service, important information, problem solving guidance, or other details the customer needs.

If you want to try your hand to create operating lead magnets, these concepts are well tested. Create your client, then use the personal information derived from your client to create one or more of the following. The higher the value to the lead magnet you can add, the higher the results.

1. *The "cheat sheet."* Cheat sheets are short tips, lists or worksheets to help clients solve a particular problem. Because they are short, architecture counts so you might want to hire a professional design to make a stunning look for your cheat sheet. The cheat sheet's unique problem-solving nature makes it very compelling on its own and includes supporting details on how to solve the problem you pose on your landing page and lead magnet.
2. *Models.* Free models are extremely popular for anything, and generate lots of leads. Make sure the prototype follows, and does not supplant, what you are offering. For example, a free Facebook ad prototype or graphic creator for a Facebook profile page could be a good lead magnet, if you provide social media consulting services. It's not such a great idea to offer a template for a full social media ad campaign, as people can use it instead of your service. Templates can be in Word, Excel or any other specific application and should be designed for the target audience to cater to.
3. *Freestyle preparation.* A combination of these resources, videos, workbooks or free training through daily emails is a big lead magnet. This is especially so because you offer a similar package of training and can add a dollar value to the training. Talk of issues that your clients require multiple steps to fix. These can make the lead magnet perfect step-by-step training tools.

Social Media Marketing

4. **Swipe over files.** A swipe file is a file designed to obtain nice examples of things you need. For example, the 50 best headlines you've ever seen in an email campaign could include a swipe file of headlines from article. Swipe files offer valuable ideas which make them unique and useful.
5. **Kits tool.** Tool kits can be a little more complex to make but they can make excellent lead magnets because they are packed with materials. You may not need to use a toolkit to start completely from scratch. To complete your tool kit, you can use the existing resources, blog posts and other content. Popular tool kits contain one or two ebooks, as well as a worksheet, video, or check list.

CHAPTER THREE

Rules for Leveraging Social Media to Grow Your Business

Whether you're a social butterfly, or you're apprehensive when it comes to communicating vociferously with others in a public space, there are some implicit rules to follow in social media. This will not only allow you to improve your social media skills by increasing your following and supporters list, but it will also encourage you to exploit the power you create to eventually expand and extend your business' presence within any market or niche.

1. Know the market you are in.

The first rule for growing your business is to know your market through the power of social media. The clearer you're about your demographic target, the better your customers will be able to appeal to. The less you know about your demographic target, the less likely you will be in a position to be successful through social media.

2. Map out a plan.

It takes work to build a popular social media profile. But it does need preparation as well. You need to build a rock-solid plan to achieve any goal.

Develop your strategy for how to get from point A to point B. Will you be using ads? Those influencers? App Power? What kind of content do you want to post? How often do you get to publish it? And so forth.

3. Focus on quality of the articles over volume.

The goal is not to flood users with messages. It is not about quantity; it is about the posts content. Ensure that the messages are targeted at your market and that every single message or unique display of something important to your demographic helps you get the most momentum and adds more followers.

4. Construct true value.

The social media's all about value creation. What kind of interest do your posts deliver? Are they in a way motivational, or educational? Do they help motivate others to pursue a certain lifestyle out there.

5. Watch accounts which are high profile.

All of the Instagram influencers I've been speaking to begin by following other high profile accounts. That produced for them their first pieces of exposure. It also helped them gage what worked for those who still were at the top of their game.

6. Post and often appreciate.

Anyone who is serious about leveraging social media to grow their business needs to understand that before they get it they have to give. Genuinously like, comment and share the posts of others every single day, and develop relationships over time. That is not going to happen overnight. You can't expect them to do the same for you, if you don't give people the time of day.

7. Use the power of other influencers.

Power users and influencers will open a door to mass media. If you have the right type of profile aligned with the base of the influencer's fans, you may just achieve the right type of followers on your own. Most companies and startups use this strategy for early expansion of their reach. If you have the money, you might want to do that, but also make sure that your profile includes attractive content.

8. Don't always be there to help.

It's not always about getting promoted. If you want to exploit social media in order to develop your brand, you have to spend a great deal of time bringing attention. Whether that's inspirational value, motivational value, or entertainment value, don't always try to sell something to people at every turn or bend, otherwise you might put it off.

9. Make the buying easy for people.

When you want to dominate social media, focus on the mobile. Create a link in your profile to ensure your site has a healthy responsive design and make it easy to buy. Ensure that the purchasing process for mobile devices is streamlined so that people can simply and conveniently order whatever you're peddling for. The cheaper you make buying them, the more likely you're going to be to win the deal.

How to Use Social Media to Increase Profits

Marketing on social media is one of the most effective ways to attract new customers and to connect with current customers. Millions of people use social media every day and eventually see it as an online business proprietor's legitimate marketing option. Connecting with your customers is one of the most important reasons for using social media; you can post status and talk.

However, more business owners must use social media to attract more clients and increase their profits. The question is how to do that. It is critical to have great customer service.

You must focus on existing customers who post positive feedback with friends and families and sell their goods.

Here are some other great ways to improve your sales by increased social media traffic.

1. Have Eye-Catching Headlines: Your website needs a blog. It is there that you can draw for your niche area in readers. Then, they will be more likely to buy from your website. The headlines have to pop out when you publish every article, and make people want to click on the link.

People come across plenty of a blog post on social media, and your post needs to stand out and make people want to find your page.

2. Using Images: Videos are all the rage right now and if you want to link to your audience, share your promotional images with them. People are busy and generally would prefer to watch a quick video about your newest item or new sale promo rather than reading a long blog post. Doing a Q&A interview can also benefit fans because they are customers.

3. Give Feedback Incentives: Reviews matter, to stand out on Facebook. How many stars you have, comes up immediately on your tab. Giving the customers opportunities to give their reviews. Maybe with a review, they can get a rebate on their next purchase. We could also have their names placed in a lottery for each comment left for the items on your website. People love incentives; just tap in!

4. Infographics: People prefer to be clear and concise about the information. If you want your viewers to easily get your information or reasons for buying it, create some infographics. Some consumers spend 25 percent of their time on social media, and they will have to stop and read infographics.

5. You Need Pinterest: Right now social bookmarking, especially Pinterest, is huge. People love having their friends share their new finds. You have to equip a Pin It button on your website. That means you need images on your blog post so that people can pin and share easily.

6. Increase Visuals: Google provides those websites with higher search engine rankings which include a blend of images, videos and text. You need great visuals, to make an impact on your readers. Don't just opt for stock pictures; use pictures to draw your viewers ' attention. If you use Tumblr, they concentrate on images.

7. Engage in Conversation: You are not some elite CEO; you are a business owner who needs to convince people to buy from your product. Consumers like to put a human face on the company they endorse. Add people into your account on Twitter. Write their Facebook comments, and comment back. When they tag you on Instagram, then post a message! Be loyal to your clients.

8. Understand How to Use Facebook: Twitter is complex and complicated for some people. Taking some time and learning how to use Twitter properly is a great idea. It's a great social media tool for getting in touch with consumers and advertising your business.

Ways Businesses Can Use Social Media as a Tool for Progress

It looks as though everyone speaks of the value of social media, but very few companies profit from it. Think about your personal use of social media— ask friends for recommendations or advice, share pictures, moments of your life, and keep in touch. Very few people act as if there are programmed social media bots. So why are firms doing this?

Companies can become very legitary on social media, but it is becoming more and more difficult for customers to ask themselves: What should be next for the company? How should the company enhance its products or services? For many people it is scary but it's far more effective to tap social media than to agonize over costly surveys and focus groups.

Many people do not realize that the audience that opts for social media alternatives is the most important "focus group." These friends, fans, and supporters want you to succeed (and have a hand to help you).

The main steps in using social media as a tool for progress and advice on how to overcome them are presented here.

1. Organizations do not seek new ideas from Social Media

Consumers like to be able to influence consumer approaches, but without first being encouraged, they would not make creative recommendations. Companies must first proactively post or tweet questions that ask their customers about product ideas, marketing strategies or something else that matters. And dig deeper when people reply! Transform the initial feedback into a talk and try to create something concrete from the dialogue.

2. Organizations use Social Media Self-Serving Data

As it is generally the marketing department that manages a company's social media activity, it does not matter if most information enterprises communicate via social media about their own products or services. Facebook posts and corporate tweets do not create meaningful communications with supporters. Not everything about you! It's not all about you! Instead, enterprises should post fun competitions, polls and questions to inform their customers of their views and personalities.

3. Companies Are Strapped for Time and Labor

Many companies claim that if there were more employees or resources to focus on this, they would be better at interacting with customers in social media. While that is probably true, the error in this case fails to understand that successful contact with social media does not have to take long to be effective. In most cases, social media managers only need a little direction and concentration. Often it can help you to develop a course that is both time-consuming and manageable to meet the departments of marketing, product development or customer service.

4. Industry is receiving highly favorable social media feedback

The bulk of the positive comments they receive are overjoyed as I speak to businesses about customer reviews on social media. You will certainly help understanding what you are doing, but businesses need more than good feedback in order to help change. For more helpful feedback relevant to the particular areas explored by businesses, companies should post and tweet questions. Feedback on the question: "What new watch styles can we offer?" How helpful are the watch bands and the face designs now, rather than congratulations.

5. Companies get reviewed, and nothing happens then: normally those people who monitor social media channels in a company are not the same people who decide on their course. That means that no other interesting ideas come to be considered via social channels.

A system must be created to ensure that the ideas of the customers are passed to the decisionmakers through Facebook and Twitter to take full advantage of social media as a tool for progress. If criticism really is to bring about change, communication is important. In order to be able to add new ideas, consumers will be more likely, as they know that their proposals are transformed into reality.

Best Social Media Channels for Business Marketing

Social media was the game-changer of almost everything around us. Specific selection of prospective customers becomes better than ever with the advent of social platforms. Social media is one of the greatest technological innovations, not just in our ability to communicate but in our ability to market directly to those we want to reach.

One of the best advantages social media marketing has for companies today is its low entry barrier. Gone are the days when a company has to spend thousands of dollars in ads to meet its potential. Now you can spend as little as five dollars per week to reach your audience!

But which are the right tools for businesses to use? To create a successful social strategy you need to know how they work.

1. Facebook

With more than 1.59 billion people, Facebook is the largest mix of any media platform's demographics. It offers an exceptional platform for linking your company with prospective customers around the globe. And from the advertisement standpoint, it's the hardest to handle and it makes the best targeting possible. We use Facebook Ads to align our current customers with more than two million identical prospects which have similar features. We then move them to an opt-in page where their name and email can be collected.

2. The beauty of Twitter

Twitter lies in its potential to viralise your tweets: the more users you spread your posts and "retweet" your content, the more followers you gain. You will post news, alerts and major media outlets. Hashtags make a big difference in your posts building momentum, so pay attention to what's going on online and include specific hashtags. You can also retweet users who have lots of followers to make them more likely to follow us again.

3. LinkedIn

If you are working in a B2B industry, this is where you need to concentrate on the social media network. LinkedIn is easiest to connect with business professionals in any industry, because it allows you to target them by industry, job title, etc. As with all social media, LinkedIn places greater emphasis on building relationships than any other. Do not use a sales pitch to lead; start by building a connection. LinkedIn Groups are among the best features for enterprises. Businesses should set up Groups in their own area or sector and encourage others to enter in their target market.

4. Instagram

This common photo sharing site is used at trade shows and events. Every time you host events, there is always an incentive for the attendants to post photos to Instagram using the event hashtag. You can also offer those who participate a free giveaway or raffle.

5. Pinterest

Use this channel only when sharing great images. Given the visual nature, quality images are likely to go viral on this site. If a highly-followed member pinns your image, it has the potential to be viewed by millions. It's great to promote products, as well.

6. YouTube

It is owned by Google, aside from being the second largest search engine. But images are more likely to appear in search results when it comes to search engine optimisation than other websites. With the acquisition of YouTube by Google we use Google Hangouts On Air to interview our authors and industry leaders.

7. Today Yelp

Yelp is critical to business. If you don't have an active strategy on Yelp to build reviews, your customers may be able to do it for you soon enough. To damage your ability to build your social platform, all it takes is one poor review. Asking your customers to check on Yelp prevents any negative reviews from standing out. It is up to you who will probably be a marketing paradise for your business amongst these platforms. Just remember that you need to check not only the social media site but the compatibility it has for your business.

Tips for Making Social Media Work for Your Business

Is your business using social media to the most? Do your corporate social media work? At this point, the organization is very likely to use social media in some form. You may have LinkedIn, Facebook & Twitter Profiles, if you are like the majority of corporate owners and advertisers, but... you really need to use these resources properly. Only when you understand the nuances and the context of each site and then build an effective strategy can social media help your company.

Here are the ideas for helping you to advertise your business through social media.

1. Understand the audience: it's a significant and neglected stage. There are broad and varied social media.

Other places like Snap Chat, Tik-Tok, Instagram, Reddit, and the many fora and web sites where users are engaged and interacting are also very popular (Facebook, Twitter, LinkedIn, Pinterest, and Youtube). Even for large firms with dedicated resources, it can be an overwhelming task to try to maintain such networks.

Concentrate instead on those social networks which offer a good chance to connect with your target audience. And you must consider your audience in order to do this. Your market and industry's specific nature will have a big impact on your audience.

Dealers who sell high-quality, visually impressive products clearly have to look for their Image-sharing services at Pinterest and Instagram. If word of mouth (and for most, if not all), is essential for your business, then Twitter will likely be right for you. LinkedIn would definitely be the solution if you are to meet a business market.

This doesn't mean that you have a single social media platform to limit yourself. But you can improve your productivity and performance by knowing your audience and concentrating your attention on the most important sites.

2. Talk to your audience: there is a big difference between social media and your audience. Talk to your audience. You want to engage your audience when it comes to social media. You're just talking to people without commitment. You could be a server, and this is precisely how you are perceived by customers.

Interaction is one of the characteristics of social media, and therefore it is such a valuable marketing tool. The first step in getting your customers to chat "about" you and your business is to communicate "about" them. And you want to build dialogue if publicity, that's just what you want. Customers like it when an organization reacts to it personally, and social media helps it. To do this, you simply need to spend time and resources.

Critically, you must be able to approach your clients personally, irrespective of whether they complement your products and services or argue about them. In fact, when it comes to how you treat negative feedback, social media marketing can be still more important.

If you ignore it, negative feedback should not lead to a poor or a poor picture of your company (see tip no. 5).

3. Admit errors: it is difficult for any company to admit if a mistake has been made. When it comes to a public arena like social media, it becomes much, much more difficult. But mistake acceptance is an important factor in the successful marketing of social media.

When using social media for marketing purposes, sometimes a clear mistake can be made. Employees can post their personal and business accounts at the wrong time, become unintentionally offensive or mix up. As this is the Internet, it is unlikely that errors will go totally unexplained. It is possible that you are trying to erase the flaw and that the business will look bad.

- ❖ Recognize your errors directly, instead. Better than a fast knee-jerk reaction is a reflective, well-designed response. Organizations are often unable to cope with a social media mistake and only aggravate the situation by swift and inadequate reaction. It's better to take an extra moment to respond to your audience carefully crafted and calculated. Do not conceal the mistake.
- ❖ Do not hide the error. Even the most clever social media advertisers happen to them. Nonetheless, the worst mistake is that it does not go wrong at all. Whether you made an offensive remark or a post, criticized a customer or anything else, you must take responsibility, whether you or someone else is responsible for your account. To delete the message is important to control damage, but it is as if nothing has happened that you will hurt your reputation. Followers share updates and capture screenshots of posts to record your profile always. You can make the best decision to own your error.
- ❖ Do not push back. Do not push back. Seek not to contend that the error was not that bad, or that you are correct or wrong with your kin. It's best to make the mistake and make progress. Debating the mistake leaves your crowd still new and can further alienate your community members.

Social Media Marketing

- Be truthful. Recognize what happened and understand why you are upset about your followers. Excuse yourself sincerely and say you regret your actions to the customers. This shows that your company is responsible and cares for its customers to feel with them.

4. Be active: This is another piece of advice that may seem simple, but it is important to reinforce it. Few things are moving faster than social media speed. Therefore, you must ensure that your business is updated regularly and consistently. You will soon lose followers if you allow your business to be lax and you will not attract new followers. Semi-hearted commitment to social media marketing is no better, and often worse, than no engagement at all.

The humanisation of your brand is a necessary step in ensuring the success of your company with a strategy for social media marketing. It is key to building a strong emotional relationship with your audience, enhancing customer relationships and building a strong brand advocacy base.

If you do not connect to your clients directly, the chances of not engaging with your company have significantly increased.

If a customer phoned you, contacted you or went to your sales office to ask a question or comment, how likely are you or your worker to simply ignore it? When you have time to contact your client or potential online–you should not handle them differently. Take the time to listen, to speak and to respond. You need a centralized plan for your community to be actively involved.

5. Answer Negative Feedback: Negative feedback does not have to lead to a poor or bad image of your company, but it is possible if you ignore it. It is necessary to respond quickly and respectfully to receiving negative feedback or grievances.

Recognize the problem–don't deny it when creating your answer. Provide actionable demands like "call me on our service line at 555-555" or send us your contact information directly, and we'll be back with you straight away.

"If you give the customer a way of resolving this situation, then you will show the disconcerted customer and others your company cares for, responds promptly and works to fix the problem.

6. Customer Service Offers: Users constantly use social media for customer service and this can annoy an organization not used to having social media online support or assistance. Social customer service can be a challenge, but it can be a great chance for your business as well.

Firstly, the simple notion that social client service is being used as a norm for most businesses means that failure to provide this alternative will hinder the company. On the reverse side, however, companies that are ahead of the curve can get more accommodation and availability from their customers. Customer service in social media can thus help your marketing efforts by improving the reputation of your company.

The fact that social customer service takes place by definition on social media platforms is equally important. Any help you make consumers visible automatically, showing your company's commitment to high-quality service. The more helpful you become as a company, the more word spreads across different social networks.

However, in such situations, you must ensure that your staff takes care of customer data. While on a social platform you can address a certain problem, it may occur that your support personnel move the conversation into a more private, electronic, phone or other location.

7. Binding company performance: The final major recommendation for your social media marketing is to make a clear link to your outcomes. Company results. You not only need to know what you want with your efforts to market social media, but also whether you have succeeded. It is fairly common to track the activities of social media, but many companies do not connect these measurements to actual results.

Social Media Marketing

As it says, you can't manage it if you don't test it, and it can't be true more than it is for social media marketing. In this respect you ought to take the time to build a concise and realistic set of objectives that Social Media Marketing will help you achieve and invest in metrics and other resources to recognize your success or failure. You can change your strategies in the future and improve your social marking efforts in the future, depending on those outcomes.

You can set goals and objectives to evaluate almost any aspect in social media marketing, ranging from optimum length of blog postings to most popular tweets or hashtags, to voice sharing, and much more! Use analytical instruments to measure what works best and what doesn't work best.

Why You Should Use Social Media for Your Business

Social media is a term that is used to transform conversation into an immersive dialog with web-based and smartphone devices. This interactive dialog between organizations, communities and individuals can take place. The Internet enables millions of people to connect and also enables business owners through web-based applications to promote their businesses to people around the world.

Today, we live in a world that does not have enough traditional advertising strategies. Social media not only provides huge outreach and networking, but also enables interactivity, which for many reasons can benefit businesses. Social media offers business owners many advantages, allowing them to reach their clients and to attract more people / potential customers. A recent report by the Social Media Marketing Industry shows that social media enable companies to gain market insight, exposure and traffic.

Gain of traffic: The majority of those who have a company have realized that the expansion from the ground to the vast expansion of the internet is important for having a website.

You can easily create your company's website and allow consumers to comment on your services. By answering the customer's comments or concerns, you can link your customers and increase traffic to your site.

Social media strengthens and visibilizes this whole thing. The aim is not only to use social media to engage people, but also to direct users to the business page of your firm, which will inform users about your work and services.

Taking into consideration your clients: Perhaps the most important thing for a company can be to give business owners the opportunity to engage their customers in an entirely new way.

Social media helps you to get customized and build a relationship with your clients. By meeting your customers ' concerns and requesting their opinions, you can improve customer satisfaction while increasing the traffic for your website, which promotes your business further. You can share photos or videos through social media to update customers and potential clients on the latest events and offers of your company. This helps create a strong interaction with your customers and make them feel connected.

Increased sales: a successful, effective social media strategy that necessitate investment, and the ROI (return on investment) is what needs to be seen, as with any advertising campaign. A good social media campaign will have a positive influence on revenue as it increases your companies ' overall exposure, lets your organization or service talk to others, and makes your goods and/or services accessible to a wider public. Ultimately, the aim is, obviously, to make the user a client / sales employee. If you speak to and build confidence with your clients, this is an indication of value and familiarity for your consumers and often a product of further purchases.

Management of reputation: Anyone involved in a company knows that a single negative comment is less dangerous than anything else. As has long been stated, you lose 10 clients or potential clients for each dissatisfied vocal client. For that reason, a reputation management team to monitor social media activities requires every serious company with an online presence. It helps the company to track the level of customer service by their feedback and enables product complaints to be addressed, enhancing the overall user experience. It is very important to maintain the image of your company. Clearly, the reputation of any company can be quickly damageed by negative comments and rumours. You will help preserve your integrity and positive identity by maintaining a strong and reliable social media presence. Using social media, you will react instantaneously to potentially destructive remarks and help to maintain the reputation of your company as a great customer service.

Depending on the efficient way in which social media interacts with users, you can use social media to perform research in the field of marketing. You should make polls or surveys and invite people to review your products or services.

You can also see what your competitors will do to plan your own corporate strategies, such as which type of service or product to begin with.

Inexpensive: The social media is very cheap when compared to other tools available to individuals and companies in advertising and marketing. The tools for social media can be used for all free. Through investing a few minutes of your time on social media, you can see great advantages in visibility and purchases, and develop good relationships with your clients.

Professional assistance is required for conventional advertisement and market marketing methods. On the other hand, it is very easy and cheap to use Social Media devices.

The global reach is also necessary for the global audience to be met through standard advertising methods at an incredibly significant cost. In contrast, using social media tools offers a very cost-effective way to reach a global audience!

There's no saying how many people your content goes viral and it's quite free to reach!

The social media means getting targeted people into your business page or profile and interacting with them. To bring a consistent dialog to your page, it is important to follow common social media practices like continuous sharing, breakdowns, questions, humor, etc.

Save on advertising: you may already know the advantages and the improvement of brand awareness of banner advertising. The same applies to websites in the social media.

You can add an avatar on every social media website. It is technically your brand mascot, logo or anything else that describes your business. If people constantly see your company, products and services updated in their timeline via Facebook or Twitter, etc., you increase your brand awareness.

If you focus on social media marketing strategies, you might consider cutting your advertising budget.

In comparison, traditional advertising is a one-time investment for a single benefit, but the customers can give long-term benefits if they have a social media presence. A key part of any company's strategic plan today is the choice of the right social media platform for its growth. Facebook fan pages, for instance, are very efficient in creating a committed community. You can learn here how to create your company's Facebook page.

Large and small businesses look to social networking as a way of reaching potential customers around the world, supporting and engaging with their products and services. By creating a company website and/or using a number of social media services, like Facebook, Twitter, LinkedIn, YouTube and many more, you can begin today using social media!

CHAPTER FOUR

Essentials to Building Your Brand on Social Media

Everybody needs to know who you are in first place, whether you want to sell products, get a subscriber, persuade followers to one point or shape their hearts and minds into your cause.

The legitimacy of your company-and one of the best ways to build it, is by the wise use of the social media-is to encourage any of these acts. Indeed, recent research reveals that over the next year 71 per cent of brands plan to invest more in social media to reach new supporters and build a reputation for their brands.

Would you like to join their ranks and make the business known? Here's everything you need to know to build your brand using social media:

1. Choose networks that support your brand image

According to Reasearchers, 22 percent of Americans use social media several times a day, making it one of the best media to build their brand.

Hundreds of social networks exist, literally, but most of them don't make money on investment.

- ❖ **Facebook** is by far the best platform for fostering brand awareness, considering that almost three quarters of adults use the app. Facebook is the only way to promote the brand image. Due to its very heterogeneous user base, Facebook is a good platform to promote virtually any brand.
- ❖ **Instagram** is an excellent choice for brands which rely heavily on pictures like clothing companies and retailers. It also works particularly well for young adults.

- Although **Google+** has not taken off as many people have predicted, a great platform for reaching men in the technology industry can be, since two-thirds of the network's users are men, most of them engineering or other engineering.
- **Pinterest** is a good social network, particularly for brands that sell jewelry or clothes, for reaching women.
- Finally, **LinkedIn** is an enhanced choice for promoting corporate content and for connecting with other influencers when you operate a business-to-business company

2. Provide interesting and shareable material

It should be said to be clear, but if you are concerned to create useful content that people want to sharing, you would create a far better image for the brand instead of creating content for subjective publishing schedules or discussing the subjects you would want to read about.

Keep these principles in mind when you create social sharing content:

- Each piece of content that you share should support the image of your brand. Remember, it can be hard to pull humor away. These can be powerful tools for brand building if you are able to use memes effectively. But you don't know 100% how your audience will respond to your image, resist the tentation of creating memes or engaging in clicking strategy, which can poorly reflect your company.

- Find out what the social networks ' material is most likely to become available. Images might echo more in your audience than blog posts, but if you do not look at your data, you will not know.

Social Media Marketing

- Don't worry about using visual content. 94 percent more views are sent to the post with images. Twitter image content earns about twice the scale of text posts, while Facebook features seven more text postings.

One of the easiest ways to create social media content that supports your efforts to build your brand is to see how other jobs have succeeded, and to compile your own better versions.

Say, for example, that one of your competitors has received a positive social traction with a blog post "12 strategy for increasing website traffic." You can publish a stronger content piece on this subject instead of wasting your time building content around unproven matters. For example you can compile a post called "102 Website Traffic Increase Strategies" or you can go through a technical list of your competitors and create your own guide to learn more about how these principles can be implemented.

3. Leverage influencers

It is critical to post lethal contents to your social profiles but this is only one part of the equation. You probably lose your voice in noise if you have a relatively unknown brand. While it will ultimately take time to build your own audience by creating great content.

A much faster approach is to take advantage of the current markets in your business.

- Mention their names or cite their links in your content bits. We have some different ways of doing this. Once the content is released, influencers using Google Alerts or other alerts under their names will be able to see it.
- Tag any influencers you referenced when sharing your social media profiles with your content.
- Upon your published content, email influencers should remind them that they are cited in your research.

Social Media Marketing

All of these actions are aimed at getting them to share their content via social networking with their followers. It may take time to build relationships that lead to influence sharing, but if you produce quality content consistently, you will see your efforts.

4. Use content promotion social campaigns: in the end, remember that paid campaigns, particularly those that run through native publicity platforms, in an age of decreasing organic reach, can be one of your better ways of building your brand on social networks. Increased numbers of brands use competitions and other social media campaigns to gain visibility and lead successfully.

To benefit from this, provide valuable incentives to your audience to encourage user involvement and ensure your campaigns have value for all participants. Although social media are one of the most powerful ways of achieving new paths, it is easy to waste time or to alienate people if you do not use them properly.

That is what makes it so important to have a good social media strategy. If it is goal that the existing influencers of social media regularly post broad content and leverage the power, the efforts to build the brand will pay off on a long-term basis.

Advantages of Social Media Marketing for Your Business

Imagine spending 6 hours a week to boost the visibility, traffic and profits of your company at little to no expense. That's right! That's right! Around 90% of advertisers have reported that social media has created tremendous visibility, and this is only one of their many gains.

Social networks are now a significant part of all marketing strategies, and social media benefits are so strong that anyone who does not use this economic resource does not lack a great deal of opportunities for marketing.

It is easy to see that social media marketing is an important element for marketing success and many marketers use the platform to realize the potential for growth. Nonetheless, some of these practitioners do not know what strategies to use and whether they are successful. About 96% of advertisers are currently involved in social media marketing, according to Social Media Examiner, but 85% of participants are not sure which apps are better used. With our help, we reduce confusion by explaining thoroughly how your company uses social media to market.

1. Enhanced brand awareness: Social media is one of the most cost-effective digital marketing methods used to combine content and increase visibility for your business. A social media strategy will greatly boost your brand awareness when you target a large customer audience. Create social media profiles for your company and start interacting with others to start with.

Get your website "want" and "post" from staff, business partners and supporters. It will increase brand awareness and start building your credibility as a business simply by having people interact with your content. Each post that is shared is introduced to a new personal network that can lead to potential customers, and the more people that know about your business, the better. More than 91 percent say their social marketing activities have raised their visibility significantly by spending just a few hours a week. There is no question that merely having a social media account can benefit the reputation and can create a broad audience for your business on a regular basis.

2. Further incoming traffic: The incoming traffic is limited to your normal clients without selling your business via social media. People who know your brand will typically look for the same keywords that you already use. You would find it much harder to meet someone outside your traditional city without using social media as part of your marketing strategy.

Each social media profile you include is a gateway to your web site, and any content that you post is yet another way of acquiring a new client. Social networks are a melting pot of various types and behaviors of people.

There are different needs and ways of thinking with different people.

Synchronizing your content on as many platforms as possible enables these people to reach your company organically. For example, someone in an elderly consumer demographic might be looking for your website with a specific Facebook keyword, but a millennium might begin their search with an entirely different social media platform, because they are looking for products completely differently. You will potentially expose the business to a wider range of flexible customers around the globe through selling on social media.

3. Enhanced search engine rankings: Although social media posts might make some site traffic available to your business, more effort is required to achieve substantial results. The optimization of the search engine is very important to achieve higher rankings in your business website and to get traffic.

While Social Media does not increase the rankings of search engines directly, social media examiners state that over 58% of marketers who use social media for a year or longer still see better rankings of search engines. If you can position your keywords at the top, your traffic will be revolutionized and positive results will continue for your business.

Let's face it, everyone uses Google to find details and you probably won't be on page 1 because your comment is usually on the first results page. If you are not ranked at the top of your business website search engine results, your search engine optimisation strategy should probably be adapted. Creates quality content that integrates your targeted keywords to give you the best chance to better ranking through social media. Content such as blogs, information photographs, case studies, business information and staff photos will create a fascinating and credible social media profile for your business. Once you start posting quality contents, you start building a social media community where people like your content and share it. Most importantly, it offers more opportunities for industry influencers to talk about and link back to your business, which will contribute to increasing search engine rankings directly.

4. Increased conversion rates: your business gains more conversion opportunities with greater visibility. The audiences may be directed to the website of your business by any message, photograph, video or comment page. Social media marketing allows your business with a humanizing factor to give a positive impression. As marketers interactively exchange content, react and post social media data, they personify a brand.

Individuals rather than businesses tend to do business with others. More than 51% of marketers said that it was good sales results to develop relations with consumers. The better you feel about a client, the more likely your company is if you have a need for your goods or services.

Research also shows that the lead-to-close performance of social media is 100 percent higher than the product of advertisement.

When a brand is interactive online, consumers who follow the accounts of your brand often begin to trust your company more fully. People use social media for their family, friends and groups to stay connected.

Why not throw your brand in the mix because people are talking already? Most importantly, if your goods or services are desired, they mention your brand to a friend and eventually they provide your business with social proof. As Social Media Examiner states, nearly 66 percent of advertisers have seen the lead generation gains at least 6 hours a week through the use of social media platforms. Placing your brand in an area where people share, like and chat can only increase the existing traffic conversion rates.

5. Better customer satisfaction: Social media is a communication and networking platform. It is important for your company to be humanized through these platforms. Customers are informed that they provide a personalized response rather than an instant reply when posting comments on your sites. Each comment can be acknowledged that you are aware of the needs of your visitors and are committed to providing the best experience.

Every client contact with your company's social media accounts is a chance to show your clients publicly. Whether a question or issue is raised by someone, social media may address the problem by constructive communication. An intrinsically positive light will be seen for the brand dedicated to customer satisfaction that takes time to compose personal messages, even when answering a customer complaint.

6. Increased brand loyalty: The creation of a loyal customer base is one of the main objectives of almost all corporations. Given that customer satisfaction and loyalty usually come together, it is important that consumers are engaged regularly and that a bond with them is developed. Social media is not just about promoting the products and advertising activities of your brand. Such channels are perceived by consumers as a support portal for direct communication with the product. The generation of the millennium is known for the most loyal customers of all brands.

Born from the early 1980s to the early 2000s, millennia are traditionally the largest generation— and will quickly dominate the market completely. Studies show that this consumer group is 62% faithful to advertisers directly involved in social media. As these technology natives need communication with their brands, companies need social media marketing to bring their most influential consumers to the attention of them.

7. More brand authority: both customer satisfaction and brand loyalty play a role in making the company more rewarding. It makes you more credible when your consumers see your company posting on the social media, in particular answering customers and posting original content. Interacting regularly with customers shows that your organization is concerned with customer satisfaction and can answer any queries it may have.

Satisfied customers want to share the knowledge about a fantastic product or service, and often turn to social media for feedback. With customers who mention your company in social media, they will advertise your company and show your value and authority to new visitors. Once you get a few satisfied customers who have a good buying experience, you can have the advertising done by actual customers who loved the product or service.

8. Cost-effective: The most cost-effective part of a publicity strategy could be social media marketing. Register and create a profile are free of charge for nearly every social networking platform, and any paid promotion in which you choose to invest has a relative low cost compared to other marketing tactics. Return on the investment and keep a larger budget for further marketing and corporate expenses is such an advantage. You will always start small to see what you should expect if you decide to use paid social media advertising. You can adjust your strategy more comfortably and try to raise your budget. You can only significantly increase your conversion rate by spending a small amount of time and money and get the investment return on the money you initially invested.

9. Gain insight into the market: one of the most important benefits of social media is the insight into the marketplace. What better way to understand the customers ' opinions and desires than to speak to them directly? You can see the interests and opinions of customers by monitoring the activity of your profile, if your business doesn't have a presence in the social media.

Social media will help you collect information to help you understand the business by using social media as a supplementary research tool. Once you have a great deal of experience, you can use more tools to evaluate consumer trends. The ability to segment your content syndication lists based on the subject is another insightful aspect of social media marketing and to identify which content types create the most impressions. These tools enable you to measure transactions on different social media platforms based on posts to find the perfect combination for revenue generation.

10. Thought Leadership: Making your social media knowledgeable and well-written content is an excellent way to become an expert and a leader in this field. This requires work to be sponsored by online networking resources, but there is no way to become thought leaders. Make sure you use social media platforms to build up your profile to develop yourself as an expert. Connect, share and promote your power with your audience. Be communicative.

When your social media campaign matches other marketing efforts, your expertise is underlined and your supporters are looking after you. Capacity to connect directly with your clients builds a connection they trust and allows you to play a significant role in your field.

It is clear that the advantages of social media marketing are so if your company does not already have the right profiles, then create them! Full the details for your client and add any welcoming material to help you. As mentioned, request that you "heart" and "post" your page to help build your profile for your business.

Consistent notifications would lead to an increasing traffic, stronger SEO, higher conversion rates, increased brand loyalty and much more through the right social media marketing approach. There are almost no reasons why social media should not be incorporated into your marketing strategy. Since it is so economic, nothing can be lost. Your contest is probably on social media already, so don't let them take your potential customers. The faster you begin, the quicker your company will develop.

Tips to Quickly Master Social Media For Businesses & Entrepreneurs

Many of the Social Media strategy have been written. Alone in the last month, all from the promotion and management of Facebook Messenger social media pages through to the production of excellent content and the development of microfluors.

A more general approach to social media for companies and businessmen is one aspect which is often missed in depth. What are businesses supposed to think about? How can companies feel good about investing in long-term trends? Which makes social media content very good?

1. Commit yourself on social media

First of all, businesses and businessmen have a dedication on social media to find success. Social media can be a real challenge, as with any other form of marketing for companies. It is difficult to grow a public, create great content and increase commitment. After only a few months, we all too often see companies leaving the social media.

We also learned that a social hang often takes eight months to a year. Not only for a clear source of content, but also to find out what is resonant to your market and what they are not. Everything begins with planning. Develop and write up a social media strategy to keep the business accountable.

A basic mission statement, content plan and goals should be included in your strategy. Above all, a strong statement on' why,' what kind of content you plan to make, share, and what you think you will accomplish in social media.

2. Show your character

The other advice for companies and businessmen in social media is to always be you (authentic) in social media.

Take a second to focus on social media companies you follow.... What's special about them? What makes you follow them? Chances are that the material they post or the way it is written is something unique. We think that they're a human, and that they don't just put out content through model robots.

The production of a strong social media presence does not just mean showing the followers the importance of your product or service. The relation and the experiences are at stake. There are the best labels of their followers in general.

3. Instead of promoting customers

The #3 tip is that great social media programs are built to listen and not promote customers. We think of it as an incredible, open-ended platform for social media, which companies can use in communication and communication with customers. That is why we encourage you to use it like that!

Social media is becoming and users expect to receive a customer service channel. The difficult part is, the more participation you get in society and, in effect, the more comments you make. So prepare your fans to receive an influx of love!

On the other hand, the customers are the most motivational source of content. Most companies simply look at their frequently asked questions or what people are asking about social media on an infinite road of marketing suggestions. When you keep on posting, look for suggestions first of all for your clients.

Also you can hear the consumers of the rival as amusing as that. All these programs are great places for finding what works in your industry, like Twitter List, Facebook Pages to watch, Google Keyword Planner and YouTube.

4. Focus on a select network

Social networks are like brilliant new objects. We would like to be all over at once and try it all because we are sure this network is the only one for us. But we are all resource-conscious, in reality. So you're setting yourself up for a long time if you try to focus on many social networks.

We were trying! We tried! We've been everywhere at one time. In addition to the less established networks including Anchor, Beme, Tumblr and whale we were in all regular networks. What we found was that we got average overall results. This took entire days to publish content on each website, not to mention. It was not viable. It was not sustainable.

It may seem contrary, but it concentrates all your resources on the two or three channels that will give you the best return on investment. Every platform requires unique content.

For examples, let's say we're writing a social media marketing blog post. The copy that you compose is a lot different from what runs on Facebook, which varies significantly from what works on Instagram, Snapchat, or Twitter. It's like an obsession with a specific platform that lets you tackle successful tactics.

5. Remember that success follows passion

The final indication that passion helps create great and unforgettable content is the social media "strategy" for business and entrepreneurs. Only by fulfilling your desire can you maintain a long-lasting dedication and social media are not burdened. Social media is good because your posts must not be directly related to your brand or business. This means it must not be what all others do.

As business owners, we recommend you choose a subject they enjoy and really appreciate.

6. Experiment with video marketing

Video marketing is one of the most popular topics in social media right now and so we would love to share some strategies you can use to create great video content.

Video marketing is a great experience for you.

Some salespeople tell us they're trying to create video of "what." The best solution we have for you is to continue with what happens when it comes to "what." Sort the blog material to most of the visitors and make videos about them.

Again, use Facebook pages to see what type of videos are created by your competitors and create themes based on this. Use the resources of your customers. See your favorite brands outside of your particular industry. The important thing is to begin with what works and gain trust.

Best Practice: There are some theoretical considerations with which people can interact more often as far as video best practices are concerned. One is the time of the recording. The most attractive videos on Facebook, for instance, are 60-90 seconds. Between 30-60 seconds is the second highest. For Twitter, the same applies. Keep your videos short and timely. If you want, you save the best first.

Social Media Marketing

You will need a good valiant microphone, natural light from a window, and a tripod, if you're going to show a person (or a group of people) in your video. When creating a high quality video, tone, lighting and camera stabilization are important.

7. Get the most out of your content

Making the most out of your content is one of the key elements in social media marketing. Companies and developers have so much going at once that it can quickly be missed that brand new content does not always need to be sent out constantly to be successful.

The more you can reconstruct and refresh your content in a variety of ways, the less content you have to give and the more success you will have. Experiment with the creation of shareable graphics on Twitter, Facebook or LinkedIn throughout your post. Instagram Stories can also be created to help promote the post. And try creating a brief Facebook video that describes the post (or even a more detailed YouTube video!)

At least 2-3 other bits of share content in each piece of content you make should go with it. That way the video could do if the connection doesn't connect. Or if the video is short, perhaps it's good stories for Instagram.

8. Boost organic content for a target audience

What is unique about social media for organizations is that you do not need to be an expert for ads to thrive. You can spend a lot of money on paid advertising unless you have a team with your social ads or you can spend a lot of time running experiments.

Our way of thinking is that organic social networks are the ideal testing ground (traditional posting) for paid advertisements and updates. In other words, to decide the posts that you should bring behind you is organic power.

The best part is that within certain social platform marketing administrators, you will target specific people. For example, let us say that your aim is to make traffic to your website.

You will build a crowd that will also appreciate this message. It might be a Lookalike audience similar to your visitors to your website. Or perhaps it's a market that has shown curiosity in your rivals. It may also be a demographic based on population data, such as location, age or type of mobile device.

Those who are already familiar with your brand can then exclude the traffic to your site.

Creative Ways to Boost Your Social Media Strategy

While companies and policy analysts have been recently critical, social media networks remain some of the most powerful and cohesive Web channels. The number of people using social media networks is over 2,5 billion and will continue to increase in the years to come.

marketers need to rely more on channels such as Instagram, Facebook and Snapchat than just hashtags and emojis. A number of sophisticated strategies for articulating a particular worldview that boosts brand awareness, drives new businesses and delights followers are used by the world's best social media manufacturers.

Find this innovative approach by adopting the strategies employed by elite social media marketers to boost the social media performance significantly.

1. Build a multi-channel approach

Facebook was the perfect platform for social media advertisers only a few years ago. Facebook then took the mantle for advertisers as the best social network. Today, most marketers seem to prefer to reach Instagram users.

There is no question, in future, which social media network social media marketers will love. Marketers should acknowledge that concentrating only on one social network is dangerous. Marketers should instead develop an awareness of the target audience. For various purposes many people are using a range of networks.

Similarly, the multichannel approach to targeting customers and clients is needed by social media marketers. Encourage users to pursue their company through apps using each channel in unique ways.

2. Engaging in marketing influencers

A recent study found that nearly 95 percent of marketers engaging in marketing influencing think it is successful. Some of the biggest brands in the world, including Adidas, KitchenAid and Rolex, are reliant on affecting content for social media users.

Internet users are increasingly worried about traditional ads. So much so that users developed "ad blindness," in which display announcements on social networks were simply ignored.

Some brands counter this by building relationships with target audiences on content that has been sponsored by social media influencers.

3. Commentators active as fast as possible

Most social media platforms employ software to classify the news and information that is prominently displayed. The primary determining factor of what content should and should not be shown in Facebook and Instagram uses "engagement."

Comments are one of the main forms of participation. Further comments in social media feeds and adventure sites such as the Instagram Exploring account are often shown.

To inspire your target audience members to engage in meaningful ways with your content, have a dashboard for social media ready to respond to user comments. As soon as you respond to the feedback, other users are more likely to interact with your posts. If you can comment in a way that feels brand and unique, your target audience can even improve brand feeling.

4. Extending reach by looking-alike audiences

Great social media marketing is not only dependent on organic content to increase reach. Some paying elements should also be included in order to increase scope, particularly once a specific plan has been drawn up.

Look-alike viewers rely on social network algorithms to help you to relate to users that are like your ideal client profile. Just upload your best customers ' list of email addresses into a platform like Facebook and Facebook will identify other demographically and psychographically similar users.

Then you can execute ads to lead viewers to your website or company page. In due course, this approach allows you to rapidly develop healthy social media.

5. Measuring on-site and on-site evaluation campaign results

Statistics are the best way to understand how the marketing strategy works. Naturally, measuring metrics, such as growth, commitment and distribution, on the platform is best. But the performance on site should also be measured.

For example, can you bring users on social networks to your website who engage with your brand? If so, how do visitors to this website conduct themselves? Are they quitting the page right away, or are they deeply researching content?

You'll know whether your existing strategy will lead to meaningful business results depending on what you are using a tool like Google Analytics.

6. Create a consistent and recognizable identity for the brand

Social networks are crowded places where people constantly reassess what they do and don't want social media feeds for themselves. For this reason, a clear and compelling brand identity is crucial to your organization. Otherwise, your presence in the social media will simply be a result of a different brand.

Develop a strategy, using a mix of media content to tell a cohesive story, which articulates a clear and unique brand identity in new ways.

7. Find creative ways of delighting people

The average person shares with 9 other people a positive customer service experience. Finding creative ways to delight users of social media is a great way to build organic follow-up by enhancing and speaking.

Develop an editorial calendar to ensure that you bring enjoyable moments to your organization and to your followers. The obvious chance to do so is at major world events and vacations, but simply developing an entertaining and on - the-shelf mid-week video can be an excellent way to make social media users happy.

The landscape of social media changes constantly, as well as marketing tactics. Nevertheless, the techniques discussed in this book remain the same whilst the tactics change.

Develop a multi-channel strategy for social media that articulates your brand voice, uses a mix of paid and organic resources and gives followers pleasure. You must eventually develop meaningful social media that will lead your business.

Do's and 4 Don'ts for Businesses Using Social Media

As an entrepreneur, you know the value of social media as a way to connect your company with your customers. As potential customers seek a new product or service, they usually begin their quest for social media to learn more about their business and to find out what other customers say about a company or organization.

While social media strategies are created in their marketing by more companies, not each strategy is effective. If you want to ensure a more effective strategy, this is the media company strategist who has outlined certain social media strategies to be used and resisted by companies.

➢ **Know who you are**

Understand your identity, the identity of your brand and the voice of who speaks on any social media site. You know your product, your development, your business or your brand best. The first thing I suggest to consumers to be able to communicate is so that people get a sense of who communicates on whatever forum they use. The rest of the strategies are written in english and you can take a word from Snapchat, Instagram and Facebook.

➢ **Don't hesitate until after that**

Without a sense of what's next, do not want to discover yourself or react to a disagreement, in a way that doesn't seem to come from the same person who changed or tweeted your status. When you say one really enticing thing, you might get into a lot of trouble, but you can not repeat it. Another problem is whether what you say contradicts what you do.

➢ **Understand your audience**

Understanding who you are approaching is critical. What are they doing? What are they doing? When are they going to live online? You will be able to figure out these issues with a professional social media expert. Knowing your goals will let you see how your successes and failures work-social media makes you see it sooner.

➢ **Don't take your audience for granted**

It's a mistake to think your audience will be behaving in some way just because you believe they should. Be a subject and not an item for your audience. Your social media work is a dialog between you and that person.

See how the response shifts. Get to know them by communicating regularly with your social media team. We are the leading people who can help you understand what happens and what doesn't-what people actually do and what we can't care less. This is a chance to understand quickly how your brand is received.

> **Plan ahead**

If you're an experienced social media strategist yourself, the energy and the cost of getting someone to know you are probably worth bringing. To measure your goals, you need someone who is tucked away within these platforms. Whether your team is extremely experienced or not, a good strategy will make you a great place to perform.

6. Create a clear and unique brand identity

Don't assume that you know everything about this with your presence on social media: having a personal account isn't exactly what Facebook ads and Twitter-promoted posts are capable of doing. As these sites continually improve and adjust these particular things, a contact specialist will help you save you a great deal of heartbreak in the future. It allows someone to keep up to date with what's going on.

7. Adopt a technique test and learn

Continue with your waterscreen test team of strategists and social media. Set out a variety of ideas to see what appeals and what does not fit with your crowd. The more you check your idea and see if that is confirmed with viewer data— which you can easily obtain from social media platforms— the more features you can build. Understand what happens and spend from not doing anything.

8. Don't get comfortable

You want to ensure you engage with other people in a creative experiment. I wouldn't have friends to go on Fridays, if I'm out with friends each Friday and tell the same thing again and again. You want to continue to engage and build relationships with the societies concerned. You should grasp the broad streams of everything you are involved in, so that you will stay important to your company.

Finally, take a look at your social media strategy and, if necessary, make changes and additions. Be mindful that social media can make your business or ruin it. You want to use to make people come to you and your company with the tactics.

CHAPTER FIVE

Steps to Productive Business Use of Social Media

Most startups, and many big businesses, still don't have a clue on how to use social media productively for marketing their business. They randomly churn for hours a day on a couple of their favorite social media platforms, with little thought given to goals, objectives, or metrics; and ultimately give up and fall back to traditional marketing approaches.

The first thing that most companies need to realize is that the process and framework for making social media marketing work are different from traditional marketing, and trial and error certainly doesn't work.

1. Focus on desired outcomes first

Valid social media objectives for a business should include one or more of the following: increased brand awareness, lead generation, service and support, or reputation management. Obviously, the platforms and how you use social media would be different for lead generation versus service and support.

2. Incorporate brand personality and voice

Popular BPOP +0% culture these days expects a more humanized brand voice, and constituents are listening carefully to the tone, vision, and expertise of that voice. Think about how you can project the voice you want, and make sure it is consistently used by all team members across all platforms used.

3. Identify the smallest segments possible of your constituents

Due to the information overload felt by consumers today, marketing at the generic segment level no longer works. Social media is the only one which allows you to be hyper-granular and drill down to micro-segments, to dramatically improve engagement levels and conversion ratios.

4. Identify the communities for these micro-segments

Traditionally, community implied a physical grouping, but today a community is characterized by what they value, more than proximity. More important than finding a community, is creating one, with your blog and other social media engagement. The best communities then become your advocate.

5. Identify the influencers of these communities

Social media brings all the aspects of important influencers these days, including peer pressure, authority, credibility, and in some cases, celebrities. Because feedback from social media operates in real time, you don't have to wait months for results. You spend the months influencing the influencers.

6. Create an action plan with metrics

Good action plans include a listening plan, channel plan, SEO plan, and a content creation plan, with activities and metrics. Social media activities span the gamut from curation to gifting, building relationships and groups, blogging, service actions, to lead conversion. Pick the ones that fit your desired outcome.

7. Iteratively execute and measure results

Measuring is all about return-on-investment (ROI). This can be customer acquisition cost, revenue growth, profit, or whatever other parameters are key to your success. Iterate and expect to pivot, based on results, because you can't get it all right the first time. This is not trial and error.

In fact, marketing in the social media is fundamentally different from conventional marketing. The depth in which connections can be made with the "audience" or "customers" is far greater than it possibly can be with any other medium. The very nature of influence at this level mans that values and vision must be in tune.

Tips to Grow Your Business Using Social Media

In today's market, it is important to harness the power of social media to grow your business and your brand. I found that there are no ends to the new opportunities offered by a carefully managed social media campaign from my Instagram postings to my Twitter announcements. In this sense, a business manager or aspiring entrepreneur who has not yet experimented with the power of social media must begin work to build a stronger online presence. I saw this add great value for my own company and great value for other people with whom I worked on the market. From my research, here are the best tips I find that can support any company to improve its visibility and activity in social media.

1. Be consistent:

Bear in mind continuity when it comes to your messages, your video and how often you use social media. In every social media campaign, it is truly the key to success. Make a plan for what you will post, and how many times you will post and stick to it. Ideally, it should be a couple hours a day or week, depending on your priorities. You cannot post once a month or five days a day, then return to demand a follow-up.

2. Use all social networks

You may be able to use all the social networks, but this doesn't mean that all your fans feel like this. You need to post through all networks if you want social media to be through. It ensures that all major social media networks like Instagram, LinkedIn, Facebook and Instagraph have a bank account and retain it.

3. Optimizing content for each platform

Keeping accounts across all the major social media platforms doesn't mean posting the same thing every day on four different websites. It ensures that the contents for each site are explicitly formatted.

Social Media Marketing

You need Instagram photos and lengthy LinkedIn messages, Youtube videos and memoirs as well as short and snappy Twitter ads. Even if they send the same note, both posts should be different.

4. Take advantage of these networks that work very well

Some networks are better than others. You really need to move the network onto and seize the opportunity if you think it fits for your specific business style and specific customer type.

5. Make sure your content is in line with your message

It is nice to get loved and follow when it comes to building a strong presence in the social media. Nonetheless, it's more than the amount of replies that each post gets. You may be tempted to upload a post that clearly attracts much exposure, but does not do anything for your brand if you do not guarantee that the content fits your message. All must fit into your brand identity and promote what you try to tell the world.

6. Some important content won't be popular, but you still need to post it

There are several kinds of contents that typical of the contents do not get much liking and share, including testaments, Charity Posts, media and important blog posts. Some important contents are not popular, but you still have to post them. These are truly important elements when it comes to determining the brand value, however, they are not the sort of posts that are typically really important. Just because it's not like this kind of content or shares doesn't mean you shouldn't post it. It might not be popular, but it helps to build your business.

7. Find a balance between popularity and business

Your social media site will be about your business, but you still want to make sure it gets the attention you want. Just put, you want social media popularity. However, the balance between popularity and business needs to be found. You have to get a bit of both and combine this more fun side, which is popular with the serious and informative side, which boosts your business ' reputation.

8. You can use social media to boost all your advertising and marketing efforts
Beyond your social media campaign you will have corporate and marketing plans. A successful marketing plan is, after all, diverse and robust. Only your efforts are complemented and made more successful by a strong social media plan. The app will assist with almost all facets of your marketing plan— and now something that you must do. It is inexpensive and yet largely unused.

Social Media marketing Secrets That No Marketer Will Admit To

I can certainly tell you how relevant how powerful social media marketing is when talking to every real online marketer. Speak to an elderly user and they will typically let you know how worthless it is.

With obvious reasons, the first group mentioned is much more encouraging to tell you how wonderful it was for you, and not for how much technology changes the latter group, but do you think the true truth can be hidden in the centre? That sort of do!

Marketing via social media is very likely to be very successful for any kind of company with punctual delivery and excellent preparation. Any type of social media marketing had (by far) the largest proportion of respondents (summing 96%) who reported that their social media budgets were precisely the same for the next year or so. Social media marketing had the 3rd highest ROI (average) of 10 different strategies surveyed.

All this means, there are still many horrific lies that the commercialism of social media does not have a single marketer, like me.

1. Social media marketing is never really free: One of the best benefits of social media marketing for many marketers is that it is completely free.

Well, it doesn't cost you a nickel to claim your business online and post all your social media profiles, whenever you want. It doesn't cost you a nickel. The only problem is, you still have to spend a great deal of time doing this, even knowing this is free. To excel, all your pages and communities are part of you must use tons of time to write. On a periodic basis at least.

It can take hours to create great social accounts, maintain them, and be involved 40 hours per week to keep you alive. Time's right money? Start to add the hours, then thought for a while about it.

2. There's absolutely no way to predict what your success might be: No matter how confident others can say that their company, social media power and success are the ultimate secret, there's no verified way to really guarantee your success. - corporation is special, it has different demographics, different history, different mentality and its competitive landscape. This is a certainty (unless you copy a product 100%). Having said that, there is no particular technique, which might be applicable to everybody. Also, keep in mind that the social media always develops with different variables and results for better and worse, so when you seem to get the better, you are always not able to predict a perfect social media campaign.

3. Once social media marketing pays off you need an insane follow-up to this: The bottom line for your social media marketing activities is ROI or return on your investment, like any form of tactic. Like most successful stories, when you run your campaigns, you can achieve good results, but your ROI is awful. This is normal. This is usual.

Hope that your next 25 followers need 30 minutes to create a good message. Imagine that you have the same post today, but you have 25,000 followers (and I think they are involved in your product or brand). It's no brainer, but which one would you believe have the highest return? Any social media actually takes a very long time to pay off.

4. Social media platforms may limit your reach: any social media firm is very keen to get its subscribers and members to pay for their advertising campaigns.

To order to achieve that, you can find that you want to limit the amount you can achieve with organic traffic (unpaid). Just because you have five thousand followers does not mean that your great post, which took you three weeks to publish, would reach all five thousand of them. Consider the power of social media. Keep this in mind. Yeah, I'm much less asking you than I am.

5. Information will never tell you all: It has an insane amount of information you will know from one of the best aspects and benefits of social media. You can study consumer behavior, community, patterns of contact, etc.

Great, but not everything will tell you about all this data combined. Such data does not provide you with insight into how consumers are thinking or comprehensive experiences with your products or services (not yet). These data cannot give you any new ideas you have not yet considered. It cannot give you real operational insights unless you ask your users the right questions.

6. Adapting to change is exciting, but incredibly tiring: social media changes more rapidly than the seasons when everything is connected to technology. New platforms are emerging and trends are coming and going faster. You really have to try to stay up (very hard if you are working alone). If you really want to survive. Even the most seasoned bloggers and social media advertisers can be very stressful when trying to keep up with social media patterns, no matter how committed you are.

You can get a routine and settle there more comfortably but unfortunately, you can't do this on social media. You can do well for a while, but believe me, if you do it correctly it never takes longer.

7. Your going to kick yourself in the ass a little more that you expected

You'll get a little more into the butt than you thought, particularly when you are on a lower level when you're in the social media world. You tend to make many or errors, typos and appear to post all the times incorrectly. This is not really important (your corresponding posts, at least). My point is that, for what you didn't do, you kick yourself in the ass.

Social Media Marketing

You would definitely miss a great chance for a good tweet, a retweet or a big deal. You will always see an entry from the competitor and think about yourself (why did I not think about it before it). In any case, your plan is never flawless these days and you must know that this is a reality.

For all the disturbing facts you hear about social media marketing today in its true nature. It is rarely mentioned. This will stay any of you should follow the most cost-effective and open Internet marketing tactics. In every stage of the business, in your company or online business, or in your target market, social media marketing will definitely help you to succeed, as long as you remember that it is beneficial and limiting.

Tips for Running Your Best Social Media Campaign Ever

A successful campaign on social media has to be prepared and a sound strategy established. Here are some ideas that will kick off your plan!

1. Start with a clear objective

You have planned to do a lot before you start a social media campaign. First, you need to determine what the campaign's main (and secondary) priorities are. You must then list the way you measure the achievement of the campaign. Some common objectives for campaigns in social media include: lead generation, direct sales and increasing awareness of brand or product.

2. Know the advertising rules of your platform

When deciding which platform(s) to run your social network, make sure there are certain guidelines for ads on that site. For instance, Facebook has very stringent rules on how you can promote your Timeline and how you choose a winner and how to contact it. Violation of these rules can lead to your full business schedule being terminated.

3. Choose the right apps to help you

Pick a selection of free and low cost software to help you run professional social networking programs. Choose the best applications for help. Of course, it's possible to run simple campaigns like "RT this post for the win" but you can pick it up with competitions, coupons, exclusive offers and branded social landing pages. Several applications are available for exploration: Shortstack, BuddyMedia

4. Don't neglect social SEO

Every social network has a search engine that enables users to find interesting issues for themselves. Until beginning your campaign, make sure that you mention the keywords that you want to identify socially and then use them in your campaign posts.

5. Support your campaign with other tactics

Many small enterprises have a strong social networking contact with their loyalest customers. However, you may want to add your social media posts with low-cost Facebook ads, LinkedIn ads, email campaigns, and other cross-propaganda tactics if one of your goals is to bring in new members of your social campaign.

5. Creates a site-specific landing page

If you want to drive traffic to a specific place on the web for a particular action in your marketing network (like filling out a web form), make sure you build a landing page. This makes visitors more comfortable because they know they are right now. It can be confusing to send visitors to your homepage because they have to find out where they can go next. Keep it as simple and the conversion rates will soar as tourists as possible.

6. Through your scope with influencers

A trustworthy, authoritative voice on a particular subject is an influencer. Social media influencers are people who have large and loyal social follow-ups in a particular industry. Create a list of players in your business who can help you spread the word about your initiative before you start a social media campaign. Just one power person's support can help you meet thousands or tens of thousands of new connections. Before reaching the influencer, make sure that your campaign helps your supporters get your best pitch.

7. Add connections to your social CRM

You can see all messages around the campaign from a dashboard using a social CRM like Nimble, regardless of the network in which private communication is going on. You can then turn your social community into a loyal client with the sales and marketing capabilities of your web CRM.

8. Measure your success

Review your success metrics throughout the whole campaign and definitely after it ends. Have you accomplished your objectives? If not, what would you have done better, you think? What looked really good to work?

9. Follow-up

It is time to follow-up with all your new contacts after your social media campaign ends. Probably during the lifetime of the campaign, you responded to tweets, posts and other updates in real time; however, it takes days, weeks, months and years to develop a lasting relationship with contacts.

You can do that via a mass e-mail (Nimble's integration with MailChimp would allow you to do this seamlessly) but a better idea is to have your sales and marketing team reach you personally through social engagement. It's easier to do that through social engagement.

Only with an effective approach can efficient social media campaigns be accomplished. The underlying promotional techniques and methods may vary depending on a certain target audience, because you have to deal with various groups of different mind. If you want to transition painlessly to new unknown business niches and product markets, go with the Nimble CRM. It's a customer service all-in - one tool that automates the lion's share of SMM routine tasks.

Ways to Win on Promoting Your Brand Content

It is difficult enough to create content that gives value to your target audience. The pressure points of your client must be established, the right way determined to convey your message and then someone (if not yourself) skilled and knowledgeable to deliver it. But there's nothing stopping things. If your content doesn't hit the market but gathers dust instead, what is the point? To get as much in the eyes as possible, you must promote your brand content.

Take a minute for the top five best practices to support the value of your company.

Why do you suggest using strategies to support brand content? Because if you want the material to meet brand targets and its intent you have to be careful about promotion.

1. Link to Social Media for Product Content Promotion: Social networks are overcrowded, and you can't just post your content and hope people will find it. You will directly target them to increase the popularity of your posts.

For example, you will discover people who promote brand content that is close to yours by using a social media management app. Take a hashtag or keyword related to content, type in it, and begin to follow up.

Then a list of the most common contents for those keywords or hashtags will be given. See who are the owners and pick their products.

You should also hit niche influencers with ample followers with a strong response and retweet rate. Your comments will most likely be used. You can also ask influencers and followers for feedback on your content using the @mention tool.

2. Commitment With the Right Community: You can easily join various online groups from a single dashboard with a powerful social media marketing resource. You can become known, build up your business experience and hit your audience by entering the niche conversation.

You can, for instance, start with your niche audience using LinkedI Groups and Facebook pages. Join the groups that are relevant to your brand content. Join the discussion, give useful advice and then (naturally) propose your content as a source of relevant information.

Online communities and Q&A sites, such as Quora, can also be used to answer questions by suggesting your content as a resource.

3. Pay for promotion: find a paid marketing tool to improve the advertising spread across various platforms. Pay for promotion: Facebook and Linkedin make it possible to deliver targeted advertisements based on location, ages, preferences, job roles and other categories, and this approach may make a significant contribution in contrast with conventional direct marketing campaigns. When you know your target well, you can use these apps.

Facebook also encourages individual tweets to be shared by consumers. This is a great way of joining the social conversation and bringing your message to the right people.

The objective of paid content promotion is to promote the use of your content by people. You want them to blog and post updates about it. Please ask your fans to let you know what they think or take a look.

4. Make use of the power of e-mail marketing: Promoting your brand content is a major advantage of e-mail marketing. To do this, you need to build a mailing list in which your friends, employers, future targets as well as business colleagues and experts are included.

You will be able to highlight your work by email–the latest and best items. For instance, on the basis of some original research, you have published a blog post although no data have been available yet. You will handle your first few hundred reads or views with email marketing.

It can also be shared (as people love to share on social media for various reasons) if it find their content interesting and enjoy it. E-mails are fast and affordable and allow e-mail marketing a big first move.

5. Conduct Manual influencers: There are numerous tools you can use to automate the search process and contact partners for a partnership. Yet you ought not to rely completely on these devices. The initial search for influencers in a market is a better practice.

Manual work is then done through Google and your ties. You shouldn't automate influencer outreach, but keep it personalized because it's much efficient. It may take time and need some precaution, but it can help you to reach out in a way that promotes meaningful relationships with the influence.

A trustworthy and friendly influencer helps you significantly by fostering your followers and peers ' brand content.

A vendor should never rely on any automation system excessively. Nevertheless, without a good social media administration program it would not be practically impossible to keep track of all the hashtags, keywords and mentions.

The formula for promoting brand content is not universal and proven. Each company uses a dramatic combination of tactics.

Implement some of the tactics above, find out what works for your company and exploration. In this way, you will find your unique formula for the results that you are looking for.

You should look to increase your promotion efforts for a successful content marketing strategy. The creation of precious and engaging content is an important part of your marketing efforts. However, companies often ignore the promotion of content that can improve their material and make it even better.

Laws of Social Media Marketing

Leveraging the power of content and social media marketing can help elevate your audience and customer base in a dramatic way. But getting started without any previous experience or insight could be challenging.

It's vital that you understand social media marketing fundamentals. From maximizing quality to increasing your online entry points, abiding by these laws will help build a foundation that will serve your customers, your brand and -- perhaps most importantly -- your bottom line.

- ❖ **The Law of Listening**

Success with social media and content marketing requires more listening and less talking. Read your target audience's online content and join discussions to learn what's important to them. Only then can you create content and spark conversations that add value rather than clutter to their lives.

- ❖ **The Law of Focus**

It's better to specialize than to be a jack-of-all-trades. A highly-focused social media and content marketing strategy intended to build a strong brand has a better chance for success than a broad strategy that attempts to be all things to all people.

❖ The Law of Quality

Quality trumps quantity. It's better to have 1,000 online connections who read, share and talk about your content with their own audiences than 10,000 connections who disappear after connecting with you the first time.

❖ The Law of Patience

Social media and content marketing success doesn't happen overnight. While it's possible to catch lightning in a bottle, it's far more likely that you'll need to commit to the long haul to achieve results.

❖ The Law of Compounding

If you publish amazing, quality content and work to build your online audience of quality followers, they'll share it with their own audiences on Twitter, Facebook, LinkedIn, their own blogs and more.

This sharing and discussing of your content opens new entry points for search engines like Google to find it in keyword searches. Those entry points could grow to hundreds or thousands of more potential ways for people to find you online.

❖ The Law of Influence

Spend time finding the online influencers in your market who have quality audiences and are likely to be interested in your products, services and business. Connect with those people and work to build relationships with them.

If you get on their radar as an authoritative, interesting source of useful information, they might share your content with their own followers, which could put you and your business in front of a huge new audience.

❖ The Law of Value

If you spend all your time on the social Web directly promoting your products and services, people will stop listening.

You must add value to the conversation. Focus less on conversions and more on creating amazing content and developing relationships with online influencers. In time, those people will become a powerful catalyst for word-of-mouth marketing for your business.

❖ The Law of Acknowledgment

You wouldn't ignore someone who reaches out to you in person so don't ignore them online. Building relationships is one of the most important parts of social media marketing success, so always acknowledge every person who reaches out to you.

❖ The Law of Accessibility

Don't publish your content and then disappear. Be available to your audience. That means you need to consistently publish content and participate in conversations. Followers online can be fickle and they won't hesitate to replace you if you disappear for weeks or months.

❖ The Law of Reciprocity

You can't expect others to share your content and talk about you if you don't do the same for them. So, a portion of the time you spend on social media should be focused on sharing and talking about content published by others.

Conclusion

Social media marketing is the way social media sites attract attention and web traffic. In order to share the content of their interests with others and create a vicious chain to cover business and extend beyond a intended market audience, creative content is generally necessary to reach the masses through advertising from third-party trust sources.

The huge, enormous World Wide Weban will support any Online Marketer with a target, product, service and purpose. If you have described these things already, then congratulations! This could definitely be the biggest part of the social media mission, and from now on any attempt will make it effective and easy to achieve these goals before you put your feet on social media master status.

The world of social media is broader and broader than ever before. This is a highly strategic marketing platform covering different cultures, genders, religions, gender, cities, desires and so on, making it the perfect way of attracting and engaging the right audience and having complete success. Video games won't concern the whole world, for instance, but only people who want video games. Maybe some of them would go and buy a pair or two from their wives if you bombard males with advertisements of high heels for sale, but a pair or 2 isn't exactly the sort of influence they desire. Thus, you are focused on certain group ages and some other factors leading to "viral" social media marketing by certain services and products, videos and news, where advertising professional and amateur people come together and put their own thoughts and plans into their own techniques. There is no university or college degree in social media marketing. This knowledge must be acquired through extensive research, constantly applied and tested in the desired field. The old tactics on TV advertising have taken it down to the online market. It is a new approach.

The proportion of people who choose to go online on a tablet or a mobile gadget over people who watch TV continues to grow every day. Statistics show that social media marketing has a lower impact than the traditional advertising approaches, but the potential it has and scope for development is definitely immense and can be enhanced and immersive much more than Television has been for decades to come.

www.ingramcontent.com/pod-product-compliance
Lightning Source LLC
Chambersburg PA
CBHW070426220526
45466CB00004B/1553